From Notes to Narrative

Chicago Guides
to *Writing,* Editing,
and Publishing

From Notes to Narrative

WRITING ETHNOGRAPHIES THAT
EVERYONE CAN READ

Kristen Ghodsee

The University of Chicago Press
Chicago and London

KRISTEN GHODSEE is professor of gender, sexuality, and women's studies at Bowdoin College and a former Guggenheim Fellow in Anthropology and Cultural Studies. She is the author of five books, most recently *Lost in Transition: Ethnographies of Everyday Life after Communism* and *The Left Side of History: World War II and the Unfulfilled Promise of Communism in Eastern Europe.*

The University of Chicago Press, Chicago 60637
The University of Chicago Press, Ltd., London
© 2016 by Kristen Ghodsee
All rights reserved. Published 2016.
Printed in the United States of America

25 24 23 22 21 20 19 18 17 16   1 2 3 4 5

ISBN-13: 978-0-226-25741-9 (cloth)
ISBN-13: 978-0-226-25755-6 (paper)
ISBN-13: 978-0-226-25769-3 (e-book)
DOI: 10.7208/chicago/9780226257693.001.0001

Library of Congress Cataloging-in-Publication Data
Names: Ghodsee, Kristen Rogheh, 1970– author.
Title: From notes to narrative : writing ethnographies that everyone can read / Kristen Ghodsee.
Other titles: Chicago guides to writing, editing, and publishing.
Description: Chicago ; London : The University of Chicago Press, 2016. | Series: Chicago guides to writing, editing, and publishing
Identifiers: LCCN 2015037639 | ISBN 9780226257419 (cloth : alk. paper) | ISBN 9780226257556 (pbk. : alk. paper) | ISBN 9780226257693 (e-book)
Subjects: LCSH: Ethnology—Authorship—Style manuals. | Communication in ethnology. | Ethnology—Methodology.
Classification: LCC GN307.7 .G464 2016 | DDC 808.06/63—dc23 LC record available at http://lccn.loc.gov/2015037639

♾ This paper meets the requirements of ANSI/NISO Z39.48-1992 (Permanence of Paper).

For Annie, Pope, and Sarah,
who taught me it's never too late
to become a better writer

Contents

Why Write Clearly?

At the end of each semester, I survey student opinions of the required books on my syllabi. "Reading [this book] was like being forced to read Facebook's terms and conditions for class," a student wrote about one of the texts I assigned. The book in question suited the course subject and contained field-changing theoretical insights. As a piece of scholarship the book excelled, winning a major award from a large professional society. As a piece of writing, however, the book failed. My students judged the prose opaque, circular, jargon-laden, and gratuitously verbose. I agreed. I prepared a lecture on the core arguments and spared my students the headaches induced by needless erudition.

University students, especially at the undergraduate level, despise inaccessible books that use language to obfuscate rather than clarify. After many years of teaching, I believe it pedagogically cruel to force students to read bad books, no matter how clever or important those books may be. I have purged many a smart ethnography from my syllabi after watching students struggle to extract the main arguments from a fog of impenetrable prose. Each year, I explore university press offerings to find well-written ethnographies. The continued production of unteachable books amazes me.

Ethnography provides a qualitative method to focus on the experience of everyday life, and ethnographers literally "write culture." Unlike any other research method in the social sciences, ethnography revels in the quotidian. Ethnographic research celebrates the diversity of worldviews that shape the social politics of local communities, making "the world safe for human differences," in the words of Ruth Benedict. In recent years, the ethnographic method spread from its original home in cultural anthropology to fields such as sociology, marketing, media studies, law, geography, criminology, education, cultural studies, history, and political science. Outside of the academic world, businesses now fund ethnographic studies of their target markets, and even the US military embraced ethnographically informed intelligence about strategic populations (with considerable controversy).[1] Yet as the ethnographic method grows in popularity, the writing of ethnography remains influenced by the widespread academic belief that smart scholarship must be difficult to read.

In the past, ethnographic texts gave popular audiences a window into other cultures. Books such as Margaret Mead's *Coming of Age in Samoa* or Ruth Benedict's *The Chrysanthemum and the Sword* shocked or enlightened general readers into reflecting on the peculiarities of their own cultural practices. The anthropologist Clifford Geertz contrasted the art of fiction with the craft of "faction," a type of writing that presents social scientific knowledge in polished and accessible prose. Today, many ethnographic books are dull and technical, brimming with neologisms and tedious theoretical digressions that obscure valuable insights. How ironic that scholars who research the intimate experiences of ordinary people cannot write for them. Scholarship that tries to make sense of human behavior—the thoughts, ideals, motivations, and worldviews of men and women operating within particular societal or cultural constraints—remains inaccessible to the subjects of that research. To be fair, academic ethnographies often serve a credentialing function, and some of the dry and uninspired prose must be blamed on rigid, stylistic norms within the traditional disciplines. But even the great sociologist C. Wright Mills questioned the pretenses of "grand theory" within his own discipline when he translated into plain English the obtuse prose of the revered Talcott Parsons.

Although some ethnographic books find homes with commercial publishers, most will come into the world through the gentle ministrations of editors at university presses. The oldest continually operating academic press in the United States is Johns Hopkins University Press, founded by Daniel Coit Gilman in 1878 with the idea of disseminating academic knowledge beyond the confines of the university classroom.[2] For the next eighty years, research universities created publishing houses to support the goal of democratic education. After the 1957 Soviet launch of the Sputnik satellite and the passage of the National Defense Education Act (NDEA), the research output of American scholars increased exponentially. To win the Cold War, the US government believed it needed to support academic knowledge production. Between 1957 and 1970, American universities and libraries received federal subsidies to fund the acquisition of scholarly books, allowing university presses to publish books ill-suited to the lists of trade publishers. Competitive markets did not promote fundamental research when it had no obvious commercial value. At this time, university presses supported the development of American arts and sciences, and the quality of the writing mattered less than the rigor of the scholarship—a golden age for authors living in the world of ideas. Of course, white men dominated this academic world, and primarily white male authors benefitted from this federal largesse.

By the late 1960s, however, priorities shifted. The American government was sending more young men off to fight in an unpopular war in Vietnam, and university campuses transformed into broiling pits of anti-Washington dissent. Federal support for higher education declined. Coincidentally, as campuses granted admission to more women and minorities and faculties grew more diverse, government dollars to support academic research and its dissemination fell further. This trend continues unabated today. University presses must look to publish more books that appeal to an audience beyond a handful of scholarly peers. Gone are the days when good scholarship alone guaranteed the publication of a monograph. Editors must also judge whether a potential title will sell enough copies to justify the investment in its production. Originality and analytic sophistication are still tantamount, but the ability to write clear and compelling prose factors into the mix, especially for first-time authors. University presses hope their books will be adopted in the lucrative college textbook market, and this means producing books that students can read. Now more than ever before would-be ethnographers must learn to write, and to write well.

Some university presses publish trade books, and trade publishers seek out talented scholars who can make their research accessible for a more broadly educated audience. Popular journalists such as Malcolm Gladwell and Nicholas Kristof get rich by translating social science research for general readers. The success of books such as *Blink*, *The Tipping Point*, and *Half the Sky* demonstrates that general readers value the insights of scholars working in fields that examine human society and culture. More important than just the marketability of these books is their potential for influencing public opinion. Books like *Freakonomics*, *Bowling Alone*, and *The Lonely Crowd* ignited massive popular debates. In 2014, the unexpected success of an 878-page Harvard University Press book about the history of economic inequality by Thomas Piketty (*Capital in the Twenty-First Century*) testified to how a well-written academic book could sway popular thinking about important social phenomena. Social science scholarship should help make sense of the world, and not only earn individual researchers tenure or promotion. To quote the ethnographer John Van Maanen:

> The ordinary truth of any research trade—ethnographic or otherwise—is that we traffic in communications, and communication implies that we intend to alter the views of our readers. From this perspective, our task is rhetorical. We attempt to convince others that we've uncovered something of note, made unusual sense of something, or, in weak form, simply represented something well. That is to say that our writing is both explicitly and implicitly designed to persuade others that we know what we're talking about and they ought therefore to pay attention to what we are saying.[3]

So why do so few ethnographers write clearly? The question perplexes me. Lack of training provides part of the explanation. In graduate school, professors concentrate on teaching ethnographic methodology: choosing a fieldsite, clearing human subjects review, identifying primary informants, ethnographic interviewing, and so forth. If apprentice ethnographers must learn a new language, hundreds of hours will be dedicated to mastering a foreign grammar and syntax. If writing gets discussed at all, instructors focus on producing fieldnotes. A plethora of books advise students on how to ethically deal with human subjects, make accurate observations about those subjects, and process those observations as ethnographic data.

When researchers return from the field, they often write theses with little guidance. Overworked professors and mentors care more about the message than the medium, and committee members will sign off on a well-researched thesis, properly situated in the existing scholarly literature, no matter how poorly the author constructed individual sentences or paragraphs. Most university professors don't consider it their job to teach English composition, and dissertations take long enough without worrying about the quality of the prose. A thesis has a limited audience anyway: four or five committee members, the student's mother, and maybe her partner. Completion matters more than elegance. *The best dissertation is a done dissertation.*

The problem arises when that dissertation has to make its way out into the world as a book. Young ethnographers face time pressure to establish themselves in the profession, either in the form of ticking tenure clocks or fierce competition for tenure-track employment. Amidst a host of new responsibilities, financial insecurity, and general upheaval, dissertations must transform into something publishable. Old mentors busy themselves with new crops of graduate students. University press editors possess limited time to counsel junior scholars trying to find a voice in their disciplines. New colleagues stagger under their own professional demands.

But bad prose is not the exclusive purview of the junior ethnographer. Many senior scholars fall into a routine of producing less-than-stellar texts. Seniority in the field provides greater ease of publication, but the ever multiplying siphons on the time of established researchers means they possess even less energy to devote to the craft of writing. If senior colleagues cannot write well or care little for the quality of writing of their students, who remains to teach the younger generation of ethnographers? The cycle repeats.

On top of this, many academics believe that smart scholarship requires the profuse deployment of disciplinary-specific jargon and what Ernest Hemingway once called "ten dollar words." Academics write, "The individual subjective experience of despondency is exacerbated upon the unexpected expiration of a progenitor," when they mean, "People grieve when they suddenly lose a parent." They believe the first sentence better expounds the intelligence of its author. This style exudes erudition, but it's pompous and needlessly complex. To be sure, disciplinary-specific jargon sometimes provides useful shorthand when conversing among professional peers. Doctors identify our ailments with medical terminology when speaking to other medical professionals, but good doctors use lay terms to explain illnesses to their patients. "Endogamous, bilateral, cross-cousin polygyny" captures a complex marriage pattern in as few words as possible, and proves invaluable when communicating with other anthropologists who study old-fashioned kinship relations. Unfortunately, scholars often deploy technical language to make an otherwise simple concept sound complex. It does nothing to enrich the world of ideas and exacerbates the insular and exclusionary nature of academic research.

Most ethnographers lack clarity on what constitutes good writing. "Few people realize how badly they write," opines William Zinsser in his classic stylebook, *On Writing Well*. Social scientists spend years mastering their disciplinary subfields but spare little time honing the language through which they communicate all of their practical and theoretical insights. Once the fieldwork is done and the fieldnotes are analyzed, students and scholars need practical guidance on how to produce the article, paper, report, thesis, or book that will be the final product of the research.

So why write clearly? I can list five good reasons:

1. You are more likely to get published. Academic presses consider the marketability of scholarly books, particularly their potential for classroom adoption at the later undergraduate and graduate levels.
2. You are more likely to be read. Well-written books attract readers. If your immediate goal is tenure and promotion, you may not give a whit whether anyone reads your book. But why live the life of the mind if not to share your ideas with as many people as possible?
3. You are more likely to influence the way people think. Social science research enhances our comprehension of cultural diversity and human behavior, and good ethnographies produce insights that can inspire empathy and understanding. Why obscure those insights with bad writing?
4. You will enhance your credibility. Younger scholars believe that circuitous erudition is a prerequisite for acceptance in the scholarly guild. But original thinking shines, even when written in the simplest of prose. Smart people can see through the smokescreen of verbiage to expose the flimsy ideas hiding behind the jargon. Writing clearly requires intellectual courage and confidence—the academic equivalent of putting your money where your mouth is.
5. You owe it to your research subjects. Ethnographic research focuses on the intimate details of daily life, and ethnographers must endeavor to make their insights accessible to the people they study (as much as possible).

In the pages that follow, I offer a step-by-step guide to producing a readable ethnography without compromising the quality or rigor of your scholarship. The advice contained here derives from my own experience as an ethnographer and writer over the last two decades; I have researched, written, and published four ethnographic books, as well as dozens of journal articles, book chapters, grant proposals, and research reports. These works have won external recognition from scholarly colleagues and peers: multiple grants and fellowships, four first-place book prizes, a best article prize, and an award for the best piece of ethnographic fiction. This doesn't mean I'm an expert, but I am someone who has spent a lot of time moving from notes to narrative.

I have also culled ideas from years of teaching and drawn lessons from my colleagues in anthropology and sociology. We all live in the world of ideas, but we need written words to communicate them. Each of the chapters contains concrete advice. Since this book focuses on *writing*, I leave theoretical and practical discussions about the genres, methods, ethics, and controversies of ethnographic research to other books, some of which are listed in the bibliography. I also don't review the constituent components of ethnographic books and articles, since this varies by discipline and is discussed at length in disciplinary specific handbooks on research methods.

These pages explore the craft of ethnographic writing, and it's the book I wish I had had as a graduate student trying to figure out how to write my dissertation and as a junior scholar struggling to transform that dissertation into a book. But all ethnographers may find something of use here, no matter what their discipline or the stage of their career. I also hope to encourage ethnographers to reengage with the public, making ethnographic knowledge relevant once again to wider social, political, and economic debates. Ethnographers have a lot to say. If only they could say it clearly.

CHAPTER I

Choose a Subject You Love

Finding a topic that will sustain your passion and commitment through the research and writing process should be Step One of any long-term project. Although a wide variety of factors influence the process of choosing a research topic (e.g., your discipline, your university, or the stage of your career), some basic parameters and considerations apply to all scholars embarking on an ethnographic research project. If you've already completed your research and you're still madly in love with it, this chapter might not apply to you, but it can help you reflect on your methodology and position as a researcher in the field. If you've completed your ethnographic research and you're stuck having to write about a topic that induces snoring, I include a specific section where I discuss how to infuse passion into your writing even when your subject matter is duller than a decorative scimitar. For those of you in the nascent stages of your next big intellectual endeavor, choosing a topic you love provides one key to writing an ethnography that everyone can read.

If you're lucky to be reading this before you head out into the field to start your ethnographic research, the first thing to ask yourself is whether you want to spend the next several years of your life thinking about this topic. A mentor may be pushing you towards a subject because it serves her own research agenda, or you may be attracted to a certain set of issues because you think they sound more important and/or relevant to the real world. In some cases, you might feel completely overwhelmed by the choice of what to study and may jump at the first topic that sounds plausible. But be careful here. Writing about ethnic cleansing sounds more serious than writing about amateur folk dancing, but both topics can provide a valuable window onto the formation of national identities. Yes, the ethnic cleansing dissertation will attract more funding, but the folk dancing thesis promises to be less depressing. You will live and breathe your topic for a long time.

Behind most well-written ethnographies lives an author who writes both knowledgeably and passionately about her subject. The thesis and dissertation are credentialing exercises. Your first book is something you have to get done before the tenure clock stops ticking. If you are an adjunct instructor or a postdoc, the book may be the ticket to a tenure-track job. For recently tenured scholars looking for a new project, the second book may be the necessary requirement for a future promotion to full professor. In all of these cases, the obvious temptation will be to choose a fashionable topic, something *au courant*, and something that you can get done in a timely manner. But the topics of your major research projects define your career. You must find something that you love to write about. Intellectual excitement vibrates through a text.

When I studied at Berkeley in the mid-1990s, the hot topic in sociology, anthropology, and political science was "civil society." After the collapse of communism in 1989, swarms of so-called democracy experts descended on the countries of Eastern Europe to teach the newly liberated citizens how to build proper civic organizations as they witnessed the total implosion of their welfare state. Western governments hurled billions of dollars in foreign assistance through the tattered remains of the Iron Curtain to encourage the development of local nongovernmental organizations. Experts lauded nonprofit activism and social entrepreneurship as silver bullets to the problems caused by the economic transition from centrally planned state socialism to free market liberal capitalism.

The political and scholarly interest around the growth of civil societies in post-totalitarian countries spawned countless opportunities for external funding to support dissertation research. In the

United States, the federal government poured money into major research universities to encourage language study and fieldwork in the former Warsaw Pact countries. Almost every lecture, seminar, symposium, or conference I attended between 1996 and 2000 focused on some aspect of civil society, and as a young scholar hoping to do research in Bulgaria, I believed that the subject of my dissertation had already been chosen for me.

But civil society never excited me. It was not only that I objected to the Americocentric zeal inherent in much of the scholarship lauding the superiority of societies with robust "third sectors," or that I doubted the messianic certainty of the political theorists who foretold a new world of "open societies"; it was that the relevant background literature put me to sleep. Structural determinism infused the whole project. Its broad generalizations ignored the thoughts and feelings of the millions of men and women caught up in the maelstrom of history. Macropolitics left me cold; I wanted to study ordinary people's lives.

When I delivered this pronouncement to my professors and graduate student colleagues, I confronted a mixture of pity and derision. They deemed my academic career prematurely handicapped by my desire to pursue an interest outside of the funding mainstream (or "maintorrent" as the case was then). Intimidated, I spent the better part of two years pondering the export potential of American 501(c) legislation to former communist countries. I wrote a Fulbright application, and my acquired ability to speak "civil societese" won me a fellowship to pay for a year's fieldwork in the Balkans. I played the game as my mentors advised.

Once I got into the field, however, my ambivalence about third sector politics overwhelmed me. Eastern Europe crawled with researchers asking questions informed by Western theories of civil society. I realized that my thesis on Bulgaria would be one of many projects grappling with similar problems. My ethnographic study would become a data point to support some abstract model constructed by political scientists. So I turned my scholarly attention to women working in the tourism sector and never looked back. My advisors and peers questioned my decision, but they disapproved from over 5,000 miles away. A few years later, when I ventured out onto the job market, I was one of the few East Europeanists not delivering a talk about civil society. Perhaps more importantly, I was told that my obvious passion and commitment toward my research swayed the decision to offer me a tenure-track position before I had even filed my dissertation.

Choosing the right topic, therefore, can make or break an ethnographer's career. In the pages that follow, I outline three major considerations that, together with passion, should guide your decision when choosing an ethnographic research project: originality; whether you stay close to home or go abroad, and whether you have ethnographic insider or outsider status.

Originality

There existed a time in social and cultural anthropology when ethnographic fieldwork meant going abroad to a supposedly primitive culture to make sense of the "natives." Thankfully, those imperialistic days are (mostly) behind us. The ethnographic method has migrated well beyond the protective boundaries of anthropology, and aspiring ethnographers can do fieldwork in any community they deem suitable for their academic interests. With the possibilities proliferating, many would-be researchers become paralyzed.

While passion proves a necessary ingredient for writing an accessible ethnography, originality is paramount. Reproducing knowledge that has already been published serves little purpose and will undermine your efforts to establish your own scholarly authority. Before diving into your participant observation, read broadly in your field of interest to get a sense of what other scholars have already done. You aren't expected to read every book in your discipline, but you must at least peruse the reviews of *all the major books* in your subfield for the last twenty years. A daunting task to be sure, but an essential one if it prevents your embarkation on a project that someone has already done. With Google Books and Amazon.com providing electronic access to even the most obscure academic titles, there is no excuse for not doing your homework before you set out into the field. Reading about your topic also tests the depths of your interest and the durability of your passion. If you remain inspired to do research after reading thousands of pages about the topic, your intended project qualifies as a keeper. If, however, you find yourself tempted to clean the bathroom rather than endure another afternoon delving into the scholarly literature, you might reconsider. Finally, exploring one potential research topic might inspire you to pursue another related but more interesting project. Your command of the background literature establishes your authority and underpins all successful ethnographies.

Originality comes in two forms: 1) writing something new about a subject that people have been studying for decades (if not centuries); or 2) writing about a completely new subject or phenomenon that no one has ever written about. Some topics and/or communities attract more scholarly attention than others. If a particular society or community enjoyed extended ethnographic attention in the past, this doesn't automatically mean that you should avoid it. It does require that you think carefully about what interests you and how you might make an original contribution to the wider literature on that society/community. This requires reading outside of your immediate field and diving into the relevant literature in other disciplines as well.

You can contribute to an established field or you can trail blaze an entirely new one, but either way make sure that your work does something that has not been done before. For instance, if you want to do fieldwork among the Kalahari San people or study the sexuality of adolescent women in Samoa, you will be walking in the large (and controversial) footsteps of Marjorie Shostak and Margaret Mead. You will not only have to read their original work, but all subsequent scholarship and criticism that followed. If, on the other hand, you are Tom Boellstorff doing an ethnography of the virtual world of Second Life, you will have few shoulders to stand on. Boellstorff helped to pioneer a new subfield of digital ethnography. The production of original knowledge provides the rationale for any thesis, dissertation, or academic book.

Staying Close to Home or Going Abroad?

Ethnographies once focused almost exclusively on the so-called "other," but domestic ethnographies have become more common in recent decades. In the United States, there are plenty of excellent ethnographic studies done by Americans. There are the classics, among them Carol Stack's *All Our Kin* and *Call to Home*, Esther Newton's *Mother Camp*, and Philippe Bourgois's *In Search of Respect*. More recently, books by Michael Goldman and Karen Ho examine the inner workings of the World Bank in Washington, DC (*Imperial Nature*) and investment bankers on Wall Street (*Liquidated*). Other domestic ethnographies, such as David Valentine's *Imagining Transgender: An Ethnography of a Category* and Ruth Gomberg-Munoz's *Labor and Legality: An Ethnography of a Mexican Immigrant Network*, grew out of fieldwork conducted by graduate students in the urban communities surrounding their doctoral institutions. Valentine earned his PhD at New York University after crisscrossing Manhattan on his bicycle to study transgender communities. Gomberg-Munoz wrote her dissertation on the illegal Mexican immigrant network in Chicago while earning her doctorate at the University of Illinois at Chicago.

The ethnic diversity in the United States provides many opportunities for ethnographers to find research projects close to home, for instance among female impersonators in the Midwest (Newton), Puerto Rican crack dealers in Manhattan (Bourgois), and investment bankers on Wall Street (Ho). In Europe, there is a long tradition of folklore studies whereby ethnographers study local indigenous populations with significantly different worldviews—ethnic and religious minorities. This was particularly true in the communist countries of Eastern Europe where travel restrictions prevented ethnographers from living abroad for any extended period of time. Doing ethnography at home, therefore, has a long history. Of course, "home" and "abroad" are relative terms, and in this era of globalization many foreign nationals study for their PhDs at universities in countries far from where they attended secondary school. For the purposes of this book, "home" refers to the country where you grew up—the culture within which you were raised.

In terms of finding a topic that inspires passion, doing ethnographic research in the country of your birth provides certain advantages. You may already possess a clear sense of the population that you want to study, perhaps because you were once a member of (or aspired to be a member of) that population. Heather Paxson, an anthropologist at MIT, conducted a fascinating study of artisanal cheese production in the United States. Her personal passion for cheese and cheese making led her across the country from Vermont to Wisconsin to California, and her 2012 book, *The Life of Cheese: Crafting Food and Value in America*, hums with intellectual excitement. Paxson studied something she loved and her scholarly curiosity is infectious. Similarly, for her 2013 book, *Not Hollywood: Independent Film at the Twilight of the American Dream*, Sherry Ortner watched 650 movies and did countless interviews with writers, directors, producers, and actors, as well as attended major US film festivals. Ortner's passion for independent cinema infuses her writing. Studying a certain artistic community provides a wonderful opportunity to become involved with that community.

A second benefit of studying closer to home is that you probably won't have to learn a foreign language. If you are dealing with an ethnic minority within your own culture, this may not hold true, but in many cases, your native tongue serves just fine. Learning a new language requires time, and ethnographic research demands near fluency and a reasonable command of local jargon. If you are not already bilingual or particularly talented in language acquisition, then operating in your mother tongue may be the way to go. Research close to home allows you to go directly to the field without spending the months (or years) necessary to master a foreign tongue, a definite advantage for those desiring not to drag out their time in graduate school or nervous about a ticking tenure clock.

Another advantage of doing a more local ethnography involves logistics. It is much easier to sort out access, accommodation, finances, and travel when you stay home. You may already have an "in" with the particular community you want to study. Most important, you don't need to arrange for a visa or a special residency permit to stay in the country for an extended period of time. In my experience from doing two long-term fieldwork projects in Bulgaria, gaining legal residency for more than ninety days involved a massive, time-consuming hassle. My colleagues who do research in Russia complain endlessly about the visa procedure, and you can't even imagine the challenges of trying to do work in countries like China or North Korea. Furthermore, getting money out of the bank at home requires a trip to the nearest ATM. When you work abroad, transferring sufficient funds and currency conversions can produce dramatic scenes worthy of the ancient Greeks.

Staying close to home may allow you to study a pressing contemporary phenomenon. If your goals include progressive social change, your chances of making a real impact increase when you challenge a familiar political system and know the rules of engagement for social activism. Many ethnographers come to care deeply about the people they study, and opportunities for Participatory Action Research (PAR) in the United States exceed those in countries such as Saudi Arabia, Zimbabwe, or Iran. If finding your passion means doing something socially meaningful, then working domestically may be the best option.

Despite all of these advantages, I always knew that I wanted to do my participant observation in a foreign country. A combination of both personal and professional reasons led me to choose Bulgaria (I haven't a drop of Bulgarian blood in my half–Puerto Rican and half-Persian body), and I've been doing ethnographic fieldwork in that country for almost nineteen years. Yes, I needed extra time to learn the language and I faced endless bureaucratic delays in acquiring long-term residency permits. But it was worth it. I love traveling to southeastern Europe twice a year, and Sofia, the capital city, has become like a second home to me. I revel in Bulgarian culture and food, and I have dearer friends in Bulgaria than in Maine.

If you don't possess a preexisting infatuation with another country, what are some of the other advantages of going abroad? Depending on the nation you choose, you may increase your chances of doing original research. Precisely because there are so many hassles associated with moving abroad for extended fieldwork, fewer ethnographers pursue this course. The more remote and inaccessible the population you study, the more likely that you will have something original to say. Furthermore, working abroad means you are in a position to popularize the work of local scholars, bringing much needed attention to intellectual work produced outside of the major research institutions in the West. Forging these kinds of linkages can be gratifying. The career of anthropologist Michael Herzfeld provides an excellent example of transnational collaborative scholarship in Greece, Italy, and most recently Thailand.[1]

There are too many examples of both classic and contemporary ethnographies based on extended international fieldwork. Some of my favorites include Paul Stoller's early work on the practices of magic, sorcery, and spirit possession among the Songhay people in the Republics of Niger and Mali. Ruth Behar's feminist classic *Translated Woman* was based on ten years of fieldwork conducted in rural Mexico and focused on the experiences of one remarkable woman who was rumored to be a witch. In Japan Amy Borovoy worked among housewives with alcoholic husbands (*The Too-Good Wife*), in Poland Elizabeth Dunn worked in a factory producing baby food to explore the social politics of privatization (*Privatizing Poland*), and in Lebanon Lara Deeb explored cultures of piety among Shi'i women (*An Enchanted Modern*). Each of these ethnographers is rooted in a specific academic discipline, but their work is also informed by geographic imaginaries called "areas."

Some scholars resist being pigeonholed onto one continent, and there exists a well-founded critique that the persistence of area studies perpetuates US aggression abroad (see Rey Chow's book, *The*

Age of the World Target). But the knowledge production that arises out of areas studies does not necessarily have to support imperialist aims. Your research can just as easily help to undermine them. Pamela Stern and Lisa Stevenson's 2006 book, *Critical Inuit Studies: An Anthology of Contemporary Artic Ethnography*, openly challenged US and Canadian cultural imperialism in the far north. Michael Goldman's 2006 multi-sited ethnography, *Imperial Nature: The World Bank and Struggles for Social Justice in the Age of Globalization*, produced a thorough indictment of the World Bank, exposing the international organization to much deserved public criticism. Passion and originality should take precedence over whether inhabitants of the ivory tower consider a certain intellectual trend "politically correct." If you discover a topic you love (whether at home or abroad), resist all attempts to talk you out of pursuing it.

Insider Versus Outsider Status

Related to the question of whether to stay at home or go abroad is the delicate matter of "insider" versus "outsider" status in the culture you choose to study. I remember once meeting a Chinese ethnographer who conducted participant observation in Waltham, a suburb of Boston. I marveled at the idea that someone would come all the way from China to study Waltham, a place I considered nondescript. I lived in nearby Belmont, and I only crossed into Waltham to purchase beer at a local liquor store. Nothing happened there. Only then did I realize the value of the outsider ethnographer. I would never think to do a study of Waltham because it was far too familiar to be examined critically.

The terms "insider" and "outsider" are difficult to define, and they inhabit opposite poles on a spectrum. A recognized member of a particular community counts as an "insider," especially if the ethnographer self-identifies with that community. In the past, most ethnographic studies were outsider studies, meaning that the researcher was previously unfamiliar with the community. This explains why so many ethnographers choose to go abroad, to expose themselves to cultures completely different than their own. Even those ethnographers who stay at home often focus on an internal other.

Today, many ethnographers decide to study their own cultures, particularly foreign-born ethnographers who are working and studying in Western Europe or the United States. Doing fieldwork in your country of origin provides an opportunity to visit home. Some ethnographers choose to do projects in the countries from where their parents' emigrated and where they still have relatives, a situation that also has some natural advantages even if the ethnographer has never spent a significant amount of time in the country before beginning his fieldwork. There are many excellent insider ethnographies conducted by expatriates returning home; for example, Olga Shevchenko's *Crisis and the Everyday in Postsocialist Moscow*, C. K. Lee's *Gender and the South China Miracle*, and Cristina Grasseni's *Developing Skill, Developing Vision: Practices of Locality at the Foot of the Alps*. There are also "insider" ethnographies like Karen Ho's *Liquidated*, where a recovering investment banker returns to study her former profession, or Ruth Behar's *An Island Called Home*, where an anthropologist returns to the country of her childhood. Finally, there are the native anthropologists who return to their home countries to work among people outside of their own original community, such as Shanshan Du's *Chopsticks Only Work in Paris: Gender Unity and Gender Equality among the Lahu in Southwest China*.

An outsider ethnography presents a different set of risks and rewards, but doing an insider study is not necessarily easier. Taking a critical distance from a familiar culture produces unique challenges, and informants may be less cooperative and forthcoming if they think you already know their history and worldview. For example, when I first started working in Bulgaria, my language skills were rudimentary. When I did interviews in Bulgarian, people spoke slowly and explained cultural practices and histories that ordinary Bulgarians would be expected to know (such as their shared history of Ottoman colonization). As my Bulgarian improved and my accent lessened, people described their past in less detail. As an experiment, I spoke Bulgarian with a more pronounced American accent with some new interviewees, and they once again elaborated on the continuing cultural impacts of the 500 years of Ottoman domination (even though their country has been independent since 1878). Although access to a community may be easier for an insider, it takes extra effort to convince informants to reflect on histories and worldviews that they believe the ethnographer shares.

Making an informed decision about your research topic means understanding the tradeoffs of staying at home or going abroad as well as being an insider or an outsider in a given community. While originality remains your prime directive, kindling a passion for your work should also factor into your choice of project. But what if you are stuck having to write up the results of a project that you despise?

WHEN THE PASSION IS LACKING

You may have hundreds of pages of fieldnotes and find yourself sitting in front of your computer uninspired by the task ahead. Several reasons might explain why you are stuck writing about a topic that barely raises your pulse, among them:

- It's too late. You have already done all of your research on a boring topic.
- You were passionate about a topic, but you have become disillusioned by your research.
- You were passionate about a topic, but another scholar has scooped you.

If you find yourself in any of these situations, you have two choices: give up on the project entirely or muddle along and do the best you can. Giving up has its advantages, but depending on how much research you have already done, you might be giving up a lot. These things must be decided individually, but you can salvage a project if you are willing to persevere.

As mentioned earlier, a lot of graduate students and junior scholars head out into the field to do research on a subject suggested by a mentor. Only later do they discover that they have no personal interest in the topic. This can be ignored when you are out in the field, but reality bites when you return and face the prospect of spending hundreds of hours writing and editing the final project. If you are coming to this book after completing your fieldwork, you may occupy this unfortunate position. In most cases, it really isn't feasible to do another extended stint of fieldwork, so you want to work with what you have. How can you make this as painless as possible?

A related circumstance occurs when you have gone into the field to study a certain population and you realize during the course of your fieldwork that they are unscrupulous and/or unpleasant. I knew a student who proposed to study a small nonprofit organization trying to promote women's health in a certain African country. The nonprofit granted her access to the daily workings of their organization in exchange for her grant writing services. The student spent months learning the ins and outs of their international operations. Over the course of her fieldwork, however, she realized that the women running the nonprofit earned generous salaries from the organization's overhead expenses; only a small portion of the money they raised helped women in Africa. The student believed the nonprofit provided a vehicle for upper-middle class white women to find meaningful employment after their children had gone to boarding school. But these women welcomed her and gave her full access to their organization. The student didn't want to write anything bad about them.

Another terrible scenario occurs when you have done a ton of research, and someone else publishes a book or an article on your exact subject. This can happen serendipitously (by an intrepid journalist, for instance), but sometimes it happens that a more senior scholar "borrows" your findings for their own work—a soul crushing violation of trust. This is more prevalent than you might imagine. In his 2015 review of Oliver Sacks's autobiography, Jerome Groopman discussed this dirty little secret of academia:

> Serving on grant review committees, I have observed senior researchers who are fair and well-intentioned, but also those who slam pro-

posals from creative investigators, then steal their ideas. Similar fratricide occurs with submitted manuscripts, with reviewers denigrating competing research so it is not published. There is an ugly side to the scientific hierarchy that comes from unchecked lust for success and fame.[2]

I had a colleague who did fieldwork and sent regular research reports back to her advisor. The reports consisted of her raw fieldnotes and daily observations of inter-ethnic relations in a politically volatile region. My friend's advisor published a paper based on her data, making an argument that my friend was hoping to develop for her own dissertation. This experience so embittered my colleague that she left academia altogether. In other cases, a scholar may borrow a core idea or argument without proper citation. Your fieldnotes remain yours, but your study is gutted without that one central theoretical insight.

If you find yourself in one of these situations, or for any other reason you must write a paper, article, or book about a topic that leaves you cold, all is not lost. You might be able to rekindle some passion for the project if you refocus your efforts on the writing process. Really good writing can salvage even the most mundane of topics. If you don't believe me, read Nicholson Baker's first novel, *The Mezzanine*, where he describes the operation of a paper towel dispenser or the mechanism of a date stamp with such luscious prose that the reader is left gobsmacked by the delicious beauty of the ordinary.

If you have become disillusioned, you can narrate that process and tell a great story. If someone else has already written about one of your key discoveries, reframe that discovery in your own compelling prose. Most academics write badly. Focusing your efforts on the craft of writing might provide a way to renew your enthusiasm for a project gone sour. Writing can be learned, and if you don't have the satisfaction of publishing the most earthshattering research results, you can at least write a well-written book.

CHAPTER 2

Put Yourself into the Data

How do you plan to speak with women's rights activists and end up talking to Christian nuns? Sociologist Katja Guenther uses a first-person narrative to transport the reader into her fieldsite and explain the presence of an unexpected interlocutor:

> When I set out to study feminist organizations in Eastern Germany since the collapse of state socialism there, I didn't expect to be interviewing nuns. Yet in Erfurt, I find myself in the company of sister Benedicta, the eighty-year-old leader of the local chapter of the Order of the Sisters of the Good Shepherd. The Order is organized around the idea that those in crisis and need sometimes need a good shepherd to guide them. With five thousand members working in 70 countries around the world, the Order seeks to minister to those who are marginalized and vulnerable, with a particular focus on women and children in crisis situations.[1]

Rather than merely telling the reader about the work of the Order, Guenther allows us to experience her own surprise at the discovery of their efforts to help women. The first-person "I" acts as an invitation to the reader, exposing the human being lurking behind the words on the printed page.

An ethnographer's observations in the field comprise the data that inform her cultural analysis, but this means different things

in different fields and at different times in your career. In all disciplines that use ethnographic methods, your perceptions form the
lens through which readers access the world you describe. Although
"there is no foolproof method for reconstructing subjective experience,"[2] your training as an ethnographer qualifies you to interpret
and represent the cultural worldviews you have studied. Disciplines
maintain different standards for so-called objectivity, and publishing formats (e.g., book, article, or research report) influence your
relative comfort level with the use of the first person. Consider, for
instance, these two contrasting definitions of ethnography, the first
from sociologist Elijah Anderson and the second from anthropologist John Van Maanen:

> [The] aim of the ethnographer's work is that it be as objective as pos-
> sible. This is not easy or simple, since it requires researchers to try to
> set aside their own values and assumptions about what is and is not
> morally acceptable—in other words, to jettison the prism through
> which they typically view a given situation. By definition one's own
> assumptions are so basic to one's perceptions that seeing their influ-
> ence may be difficult, if not impossible. Ethnographic researchers,
> however, have been trained to look for and to recognize underlying
> assumptions, their own and those of their subjects, and to try to over-
> ride the former and uncover the latter.[3]

> Ethnography is still a relatively artistic, improvised, and situated form
> of social research where the lasting tenets of research design, theo-
> retical aims, canned concepts, and technical writing have yet to leave
> a heavy mark. In the end, this is the way I think it should be, for a
> persuasive and widely read ethnography will always be something of a
> mess, a mystery, and a miracle.[4]

While Anderson asserts that the subjective experience of the ethnographer can be accounted for and controlled, Van Maanen believes
that the subjective messiness of ethnography makes the genre valuable and unique among the social sciences. There exists a long and

contested literature about the supposed objectivity of the ethnographer, but this falls outside of the purview of this book.[5] Wherever you fall on the objectivity-subjectivity spectrum, however, consider putting yourself into the data.

Junior scholars fear that exposing their presence as the researcher undermines their credibility. Anthropologist Ruth Behar captured the essence of this sentiment when she wrote: "Among anthropologists it's a mortal sin to write about oneself. We are taught to be scribes, to tell other people's stories."[6] But the judicious use of the first person brings life and vigor to any ethnographic text—it enhances your credibility because it establishes that you were there, that your knowledge derives from first-hand experience. Participant observation rests on your access to the community or culture in question, and readers want to know how you came to be accepted.

Methodology sections feel more genuine when written in a personal way. Loïc Wacquant provides an example of the use of the first person in discussing methodology. A French student of Pierre Bourdieu, Wacquant moved to the South Side of Chicago to become an apprentice boxer in an African-American gym. In the following passage, Wacquant not only explains how he learned to box, but also opens a window onto his passion for the sport and the relationships he developed in the field:

> For three years I trained alongside local boxers, both amateur and professional, at the rate of three to six sessions a week, assiduously applying myself to every phase of their rigorous preparation, from shadowboxing in front of mirrors to sparring in the ring. Much to my own surprise, and to the surprise of those close to me, I gradually got taken in by the game. . . . In the intoxication of immersion, I even thought for a while of aborting my academic career to "turn pro" and thereby remain with my friends from the gym and its coach, DeeDee Armour, who had become a second father for me.[7]

Wacquant's *Body and Soul: Notebooks of an Apprentice Boxer* engages important theoretical issues in sociology and is a smart and empirically rich ethnography complemented by interwoven first-person accounts.

The sociologist Monica McDermott experiments with a similar strategy in her book, *Working Class White*. McDermott, a white American woman, worked for a year at two gas station convenience stores in Atlanta and Boston. From her vantage point as a cashier, she observed the interracial interactions of her customers, arguing that anti-black prejudice persists in the United States many years after the civil rights victories of the 1960s. McDermott presents extensive evidence of the everyday operations of racism among the white working class, but she also gives readers a visceral sense of the precariousness of the lives of America's working poor, regardless of color. She writes:

> The crimes that I witnessed while working as a convenience store clerk for just under a year ranged from the theft of a candy bar by an adolescent to a carjacking in the parking lot; the stolen vehicle was later used in a string of armed robberies committed across the state. I was not on duty when a gunfight occurred in the parking lot of General Fuel, and a murder at a nearby pay phone occurred just after I quit working at the store. I also ended my shift at Quickie Mart just over an hour before the cashier who relieved me had a gun stuck in his face until he emptied the cash register.[8]

Now read this same paragraph rendered in the third person:

> The crimes that the ethnographer witnessed while working as a convenience store clerk for just under a year ranged from the theft of a candy bar by an adolescent to a carjacking in the parking lot; the stolen vehicle was later used in a string of armed robberies committed across the state. The ethnographer was not on duty when a gunfight occurred in the parking lot of General Fuel, and a murder at a nearby pay phone occurred just after the ethnographer quit working at the store. The ethnographer also ended her shift at Quickie Mart just over

an hour before the cashier who relieved her had a gun stuck in his face until he emptied the cash register.

The same text written in the third person may sound more "objective," but it lacks the power and intimacy of the first-person account. For some projects, too much first person might feel forced, but Wacquant and McDermott integrate the "I" without letting it overpower their work.

A more generous use of the first person can also allow you to unite disparate bits of data and observation under the umbrella of one text. In her book *Alive in the Writing: Crafting Ethnography in the Company of Chekhov*, anthropologist Kirin Narayan argues that "a writer's voice necessarily implies a self with certain sensibilities, regardless of whether the first person is used. Bring in an 'I' and set it rolling . . . , and you'll be unfurling a long thread, a thread you can then use to artfully stitch together diverse experiences and insights."[9] In other words, all authors have a personal voice inflecting their prose, whether they choose to deploy an "I" or not.

Another example comes from John Borneman's ethnography *Syrian Episodes: Sons, Fathers, and an Anthropologist in Aleppo*. Borneman traveled to Syria on the Fulbright Program, but bureaucratic intrigues prevented him from teaching at the university there. *Syrian Episodes* delves into the everyday lives of men in Aleppo, probing the various hierarchies and power relations that define Syrian masculinity. The whole book is filtered through the "I" of John Borneman, who embraces and even celebrates the subjective nature of his text. He writes:

> I suppose I went to Syria for enchantment, reenchantment, or some kind of magic unavailable to me in America, my home, and in this motivation I share something with the now largely discredited desires of some of my Orientalist predecessors: Gustave Flaubert, Ernest Renan, Richard Burton, T. E. Lawrence, Rudolph Virchow, Alexander von Humboldt, and all people from the West who go to the

East—in this case, the Near East or Middle East—for an encounter
with difference. But in this encounter we do not all have the same
kind of experience.[10]

Borneman advocates for documentary forms of ethnography, where
the experience of "being there" supersedes the substantiation of a
particular theoretical argument."This style of writing may not work
for dissertation writers or junior scholars trying to earn tenure (particularly if you don't have supportive senior colleagues willing to
accept more evocative writing styles), but once you reach a certain
point in your career, you have more freedom to experiment. *Syrian
Episodes* captures the privilege of an established ethnographer not
afraid to play with literary forms. The book (published in 2007 and
researched before the Syrian civil war began in 2011) contains many
examples of how the use of the first person can bring what otherwise might be a "dry" history to life. Consider the following passage:

> When I think of the camel, I think romantically: of its sweet and
> open face, the large, unblinking eyes and flared nostrils, its peculiar
> hump (the dromedary or Arab camel has only one), its oversize knees
> and tall spindly legs. I think of its relation to the ancient overland Silk
> Road that used to extend, from the time of its origin around 100 B.C.,
> from China through the Fertile Crescent to Rome. Beginning in the
> sixteenth century, the discovery of a sea route around the Cape of
> Good Hope reduced the importance of the Silk Road, and slowly the
> caravans of Aleppo and the camels that carried the goods from China
> to Europe and back, and the city of Aleppo itself, declined in impor-
> tance. Today, the Syrian part of the Silk Road no longer exists except
> as an imaginative topos, a source of revenue for residents who can use
> its geographical and cultural history—evoking Marco Polo, Alex-
> ander the Great, the Crusades—to lure tourists to visit. The camel's
> turn parallels this larger history of material decline and displacement
> to imaginary sites. Now and then, I see a camel on the road between
> Aleppo and Damascus, but for the most part I see them used only by
> Bedouins in the eastern part of the country, who offer me as part of

the tourist experience the opportunity to ride, or at least sit on them, for a small fee, at many of the country's archaeological sites.[12]

In this one paragraph, Borneman's imagining of the camel exposes the reader to over two thousand years of history and thousands of miles of geography. The first-person "I" renders lyrical otherwise tedious information that readers might skim over. The first person allows the reader to feel part of the author's journey of discovery.

Writing up the findings of Participatory Action Research (PAR) demands the first person, as does inserting your own opinion on how to fix a problem you've identified. Participatory Action Research refers to projects in which a scholar combines her fieldwork with an active program for social change—collaborating with community members and seeking to understand the world while attempting to transform it. Some books, such as Julie Hemment's *Empowering Women in Russia*, emerge from fieldwork conducted using explicit PAR methodology, but examples of this ethnographer activism abound. One of the most elegant instances comes from Philippe Bourgois's book, *In Search of Respect: Selling Crack in El Barrio*. Bourgois narrates in the first person throughout the book, occasionally stepping back to comment on his own presence and interactions in the field. But only in the final chapter does Bourgois reveal the extent of his emotional entanglements to the reader. He writes:

> I hope my presentation of the experience of social marginalization in El Barrio, as seen through the struggles for dignity and survival of Ray's crack dealers and their families, contributes on a concrete practical level to calling attention to the tragedy of persistent poverty and racial segregation in the urban United States. I cannot resign myself to the terrible irony that the richest industrialized nation on earth, and the greatest world power in history, confines so many of its citizens to poverty and to prison.[13]

In this passage, Bourgois breaks character and exposes the ethnographer who harbors a political commitment to improve the lives of his informants. This may appear risky to ethnographers who desire the veneer of objectivity, but writing about your own humanity, especially in the face of great injustice, can make your work more accessible to those saddled with rigid stereotypes and preconceived notions. Because Bourgois exposes the inner logics of Puerto Rican street masculinity, he transforms Cesar and Primo into "sensitive crack dealers." *In Search of Respect* has become a standard text in a variety of introductory college courses, and year after year, my own students rank the book as their favorite.

Disciplinary norms in your field dictate how and how much to put yourself in your writing, but if you maintain any say in the matter, embrace the first person and let your own voice be the reader's narrative guide.

CHAPTER 3

Incorporate Ethnographic Detail

Clifford Geertz's famous essay, "Deep Play: Notes on the Balinese Cockfight," draws the reader back to 1958 in a scene when Geertz and his wife hid from the Balinese police after attending an illegal cockfight:

> In the houseyard, the high-walled enclosures where the people live, fighting cocks are kept in wicker cages, moved frequently about so as to maintain the optimum balance of sun and shade. They are fed a special diet, which varies somewhat according to individual theories but which is mostly maize, sifted for impurities with far more care than it is when mere humans are going to eat it and offered to the animal kernel by kernel. Red pepper is stuffed down their beaks and up their anuses to give them spirit. They are bathed in the same ceremonial preparation of tepid water, medicinal herbs, flowers, and onions in which infants are bathed, and for a prize cock just about as often. Their combs are cropped, their plumage dressed, their spurs trimmed, their legs massaged, and they are inspected for flaws with the squinted concentration of a diamond merchant.[1]

In his seminal 1973 book, *The Interpretation of Cultures*, Geertz spends his first chapter discussing the importance of what he calls "thick description," an essential component of interpretive anthropology, best exemplified by his writing style in "Deep Play." Geertz believed that rituals provide a language for cultures to tell stories about themselves. Rich narrative details inform interpretive analysis as well as provide the raw material for beautiful ethnographic writing. In the one short paragraph quoted above, Geertz captures the Balinese passion for cockfighting through his careful description of the care of their roosters.

Every aspiring ethnographer must master the art of critical observation and learn how to faithfully record the minutia of daily life. Illustrating critical insights with specific observations about people, places, and events enriches any ethnographic text. Sociologist Elaine Weiner captures this sentiment beautifully:

> My favorite ethnographies are always those where I feel I can literally "hear" the data. Ethnographies, to me, are fundamentally stories and the people that they are about, in my mind, are the storytellers, in part. Writing ethnographically, as a social scientist, involves positioning these individuals' stories such that a larger narrative becomes apparent, which illuminates the interplay of various social forces and people's own agency.[2]

Writing Fieldnotes

Detailed and vibrant fieldnotes provide the foundation for a detailed and vibrant ethnography. Writing quality fieldnotes takes time and practice, but producing careful and thorough observations in the field proves invaluable when you sit down to craft a finished ethnographic paper, article, report, or book. Every novice ethnographer should read *Writing Ethnographic Fieldnotes* by Emerson, Fretz, and Shaw before embarking on their field research. In this comprehensive guide, the authors assert:

> The ethnographer's central purpose is to describe a social world and its people. But often beginning researchers produce fieldnotes lacking in sufficient and lively detail. Through inadvertent summarizing and

evaluative wording, a fieldworker fails to adequately describe what she observed and experienced.[3]

All researchers fall victim to the twin evils of "inadvertent summarizing and evaluative wording." In the rush to get everything down, we employ rhetorical shortcuts: recording the gist of a conversation, paraphrasing key quotes, ignoring body language, and so forth. Writing that someone "was angry" requires less time than describing how that person manifested his anger through action.

My filing cabinets contain hundreds of pages of fieldnotes from my first two major ethnographic research projects (including my dissertation). Reading through the earliest fieldnotes, written in 1998–2000, exposes many of my own shortcomings as a novice ethnographer. I wrote all of my dissertation fieldnotes longhand. I tried to use a tape recorder for some interviews and interactions, but many of my informants felt uncomfortable with the Dictaphone (this was postcommunist Bulgaria in the 1990s). They spoke more honestly when the recorder was switched off. I took copious notes, but failed to record details in a systematic way. I missed the trees for the forest. After fourteen months in the field, I collected enough information to write my thesis, but today I recognize that I wrote lousy fieldnotes.

When I returned to Bulgaria for a second stint of sustained fieldwork in 2005, my notes improved because I had discovered a new strategy. I took handwritten notes during the day and typed the notes into an e-mail that I sent to myself each evening. Writing this nightly e-mail provided an electronic backup and gave me the chance to fill in details that I overlooked during the day. At first the new system worked well, but it required more time. I started the fieldwork for my second project with my three-year-old daughter, and I waited until she fell asleep before I typed up my e-mail. So much occurred in any given day that I ran out of steam before I could get it all down. Since my daughter woke me each day at sunrise, I began to skip over the thick description so I could get to bed. Only after I returned to the United States did I realize I had lost hundreds, perhaps thousands, of details as a result.

Sleep and time with my daughter outweighed the imperatives of research, but reading back through these early fieldnotes reveals the shortcuts I took. There were several entries, for example, where I just noted the time of day and described an event or conversation. When I enjoyed more time to write my fieldnotes, I recorded the hour and then allowed myself to describe the lighting of the scene and the position of the sun (if I was outdoors). Were there shadows and where were they cast? Were people squinting as they talked or were they straining their eyes to see in the darkness? If I was indoors, I thought about how much artificial light there was and of what kind. Were there incandescent bulbs, and if so, how many watts? Were there standing lamps or table lamps? Was there overhead lighting, and if so, was it fluorescent?

Although this may seem like trivial information, profound observations arose from these passages. When I visited people's homes in rural Bulgaria, I could surmise much about a family's socioeconomic status by lighting. Electricity prices rose after the collapse of communism, and artificial light became a luxury. Once I was doing an interview in a private flat, and my host turned on a lamp behind me so that I could see better as I took notes. I jotted a sentence about this in my notebook. When I read it later I started to pay attention to how people managed their artificial light. A dim apartment filled with unused communist-era lamps symbolized the economic catastrophe that befell so many families after 1989. I observed this phenomenon in the field, but only came to realize its significance when analyzing my fieldnotes weeks later. One detail allowed me to see a wider pattern.

Some ethnographers transfer their fieldnotes into their final texts using block quotations, but I find that my fieldnotes are too unrefined to incorporate directly into my manuscript. I will discuss the use of fieldnotes in more detail in chapter 5, on integrating your theory, but in general I tend to write from my fieldnotes, crafting my raw ethnographic observations into more robust descriptions of people, places, and events.

Describing People

Readable ethnographies require compelling "characters." Since personal interactions in the field drive ethnographic research, present your primary informants in three-dimensions, as real people, not as caricatures. Of course, ethnographers possess an ethical obligation to change some identifying details of their research subjects (to a greater or lesser extent as required by the Institutional Review Board that approved the original research protocol), but this provides no excuse to create generic people. Because you must change details doesn't mean you should use fewer of them.

When writing about people, avoid the temptation to describe someone as a list of physical or emotional attributes: tall, fair, brave, outspoken, driven, etc. Instead, consider describing them in terms of their actions; show how they negotiate the vicissitudes of daily life. This idea of putting action before character, or that character is a function of action, dates back to Aristotle's *Poetics*: "Now character determines men's qualities, but it is by their actions that they are happy or the reverse. Dramatic action, therefore, is not with a view to the representation of character: character comes in as subsidiary to the actions."[4] No writer should ignore Aristotle's key insight, but particularly ethnographers. Whereas novelists can create rounded characters by inventing fictional deeds for them to perform, the ethnographer must deal with real people in a real world performing quotidian actions. You must capture how your "characters" function in their social universes.

This careful focus on people underpins the best ethnographies. Good ethnographic writing uses the prosaic to explore the shared practices and beliefs of a particular society. Our "characters" act in everyday, routine situations, and comparative banality exposes significant cultural similarities and differences. For instance, when Americans pose for a photograph they usually smile. Bulgarians do not always smile at the camera, and in fact, government regulations prohibit smiling in official photographs, including driver's licenses and school ID cards.

Official conventions about photography can work their way into everyday life, as can social norms about how to pose for the camera. I remember once seeing a photo of the finalists in an international beauty pageant. While the other finalists showed off their pearly whites, Miss Bulgaria kept her face stoic. Was this a conscious choice, or was the cultural convention so firmly entrenched that she didn't realize that she was the only one not smiling? In Japan, many people make peace fingers when someone points a camera lens in their direction. From the three years that I lived in Kyushu during my mid-20s, I have hundreds of photos of students and friends holding their hands up in victory "Vs" like Richard Nixon. At some point during my second year there, I started doing it, too. I don't remember making a conscious choice—it just felt wrong not to make peace fingers. I continued this habit when I returned to the States, and a keen observer surmised that I'd lived a long time in Japan.

Using small details like these enhances the way we write about people. Describing how someone reacts in a familiar situation provides an excellent window into his or her character. We know what we would do in front of a camera: smile, tilt our heads, turn sideways, or strike a skinny arm pose. Some of us hate cameras and shy away or cover our faces. Fiction writers use details like these to bring their characters to life. If I write, "Matthew was shy and had a melancholy disposition," I tell the reader about Matthew's personality. Or I can put Matthew in front of a camera and show his shyness: "Matthew was the kind of American who never smiled in photographs. When someone prompted him to 'say cheese,' he pressed his lips together and looked down at his shoes." This second sentence captures more nuances about Matthew because it describes him reacting to a familiar circumstance.

Here is another example taken from the sorts of craft books intended for fiction writers. If I want to describe a woman who gets frustrated when things happen too slowly, I might write, "Elena was an impatient woman." But fiction writers try to demonstrate Elena's impatience in action. For instance, a novelist might write:

Elena gauged the length of the different lines in the grocery store checkout lanes. She never read the headlines on the magazines. Instead, Elena assessed the contents of other people's carts to determine which line would move the fastest. She chose one line, but hopped over to a different one if she thought it was quicker. If she had a hand basket, she went through the express lane even when she had more than twelve items.

The familiarity of the situation provides the reader with a sense of Elena's character. Most of us have stood in lines at the grocery store, reading the tabloids or staring at the chocolate strategically placed to tempt us. When you are in the field, go to a market or a grocery store and watch how real people behave. Examine the social norms and expectations of grocery store etiquette. In Bulgaria and Germany, the cashiers are sitting in chairs, and the customer bags his own groceries. Rarely do cashiers converse with customers. In Maine, clients often chat with the cashiers in the checkout lane, making small talk about the weather. There are baggers, usually young high school students, who ask if you want "paper or plastic." When I lived in rural Japan, the cashiers loved to chat. They commented on the things I bought and asked what I planned to cook with certain ingredients. A cashier once mortified me when she asked if I had a bad stomach because I was buying what she considered an excessive amount of toilet paper.

If you were writing fiction, you could explore a character by imagining her in a grocery checkout line. Is she friendly to the cashiers, or is she chatting on her mobile phone? Is she someone who reads the magazines or someone who organizes coupons? My mother watches the prices of her items flash up on the register to ensure that the cashier doesn't scan the same item twice. After paying, she scrutinizes her receipt to check that there are no errors in the store's favor. I spend my time in the checkout line swatting e-mails on my smart phone and shove the cashier's receipt in my purse without a second thought. Even without looking at the contents of our carts, you can make accurate observations about who we are by observing our checkout line behavior.

Where novelists imagine, ethnographers must observe. You might find it difficult to write about people that you don't know, and we all rely on stereotypes when describing strangers. But you must endeavor to capture specificity in even the most fleeting encounter. For instance, rather than writing that a late middle-aged man is overweight, you could describe how his cheeks fell into loose jowls below his jawline, framing the bulge of his second chin. Instead of telling the reader that a man is bald, discuss the shape of his head or the shine on his scalp. Describe tall people walking through low doorways and short people stretching to grab a box of breakfast cereal on the highest shelf. Show clumsy people tripping or walking into doorframes. Describe gesticulations and posture. Remember Sherlock Holmes; he could surmise the most intimate details of people's lives by small clues in their dress or behavior.

When describing people watch out for adjectives and adverbs that describe character. If you want to say that someone spoke "meekly" or "boldly," avoid using the adverb, and tell the reader how that person spoke: "She spoke in a low, half-mumbled voice with long, tentative pauses between words." Or, "She spoke in a loud, clear voice, enunciating her consonants like she was reading a proclamation." Adjectives and adverbs may populate your fieldnotes, but when you sit down to write your final ethnographic text, circle all of these helper words and decide which ones you can replace with ethnographic details. Some adjectives cannot be replaced; for instance, a green dress is a green dress. You might choose a more specific adjective—a celadon dress—but celadon remains an adjective. Convert adjectives used to describe character, like "impatient" or "pompous," into actions.

A nice example of thick description comes from sociologist Karyn Lacy's book, *Blue-Chip Black: Race, Class, and Status in the New Black Middle Class.* On the opening page of the introduction, Lacy paints a picture of her informants by situating them in their social world:

"They're trying to be like whites instead of being who they are,"
Andrea Creighton, a forty-three-year-old information analyst with
the federal government, told me when I asked whether she believed
blacks had made it in the United States or still had a long way to
go.... She and her husband, Greg, have two teenage children: a girl,
age 17, and a boy, age 15. They have lived on a quiet street in Sherwood
Park, an upper-middle-class suburb of Washington D.C., for seven
years. Their four-bedroom home is an imposing red-brick-front colonial with shiny black shutters, nestled on an acre of neatly manicured
lawn. The children are active members of the local soccer team, and
Greg is one of the team's coaches. Andrea and her husband each drive
midsize cars and have provided their daughter, who is old enough to
drive unaccompanied by an adult, with her own car. At first blush,
they seem nearly identical to their white middle-class counter-
parts. But unlike the nearly all-white neighborhood that the average
middle-class white family calls home, the Creighton's upscale subdivision is predominantly black.[5]

Lacy curates precise details about the Creighton's lifestyle to explore
their similarity to white middle-class families, highlighting the contrast with her informant's opening statement. She deploys adjectives
(and one adverb) to describe things but not character: words like
quiet, upper-middle-class, four-bedroom, imposing, shiny, midsize,
upscale, and neatly manicured. Lacy concentrates on what her informants do. The children play soccer, the dad coaches the team, and
they bought their teenage daughter her own midsize car. They live
in an all-black subdivision and someone (the dad? hired landscap-
ers?) ensures that their lawn remains watered, weeded, and mowed.
    Before you start writing your book or article, imagine your pri-
mary informants as characters in a novel. If you were a fiction writer,
what details about their lives could you use to best describe who they
are? Examine your fieldnotes and sketch out some examples of how
your informants behave within their social milieu. Show what makes
them unique as individuals. When you have written these descrip-

tions, go back and count the number of adjectives in your text. Try to replace some adjectives with descriptions of actions. The more an ethnographer uses action to provide characterization, the more rich the reading experience for the reader. Of course, some adjectives are unavoidable, and "showing" takes a lot of extra space. Too much thick description can become tedious; there will be places where telling is more expedient than showing. Create accessible characters by allowing them possibilities for action, but don't get bogged down in long-winded descriptions that distract from the main corridor of your narrative. Strike a balance between specific detail and narrative efficiency, but give the people in your research opportunities to act within their worlds. Let them be guides to the places and events that inform your interpretive analysis.

CHAPTER 4

Describe Places and Events

Describing Places

The battered Peugeot taxi swerved to avoid a pothole, and I clung to the window crank, gazing out at the throngs of pedestrians on the crowded Abidjan city streets. Women walked with babies strapped to their backs, while they carried all manner of burdens piled high on their heads: an enamel tray of imported apples to sell in the market, an old-fashioned foot-pedal sewing machine, a vinyl pocketbook. Stationed at street corners, men dressed in brightly patterned print suits hawked gold-colored necklaces, snakeskin wallets, folding umbrellas. When would the view outside the open window reveal dirt paths winding through dense forest rather than paved roads leading from hotel to restaurant to bank?[1]

In this rich description of the capital of Cote d'Ivoire, anthropologist Alma Gottlieb brings the city to life for her reader, contrasting the paved roads with the dirt paths she hopes to see and populating the view out her taxi window with people immersed in the rhythm of their daily lives. Gottlieb does not tell us that this is West Africa, she uses carefully selected detail to show us.

Places cannot do things the same way that people can, and many beginning ethnographers fall into a purely descriptive mode when writing about physical settings. But there are similar tricks to writing about places that can enliven your prose and transport the reader into a vividly rendered world on the page. Once again, your ability to incorporate rich ethnographic detail will begin with your fieldnotes, but there are two simple technologies to help you remember details about place: always collect maps and take lots of photos.

When I am first getting settled into the field, I become an avid amateur cartographer. I draw simple sketches to figure out the lay of the land. In the beginning, these little maps prevent my getting lost, but they also serve as invaluable tools for remembering topography and spatial orientations. I also use a small point-and-shoot camera to take photos of outdoor scenes and of people in their homes when I interview them. These snapshots help me keep pseudonyms straight, but they also contain important information about the spaces where my informants live. These aren't photos to be published, but rather tools to assist my sometimes-imperfect memory. (Taking photos for publication will be discussed in chapter 7).

Once you have the raw materials of fieldnotes, photos, and maps, you can write about places in three ways:

Describe them in relation to other places
Describe their histories
Describe them in relation to the people who inhabit them

PLACES IN RELATION TO OTHER PLACES

Whether working close to home or abroad, the ethnographer must paint a picture of place for the reader. Writing about place, especially far-off lands that defy readers' imaginations, presents descriptive challenges. Comparing new places to familiar ones provides a simple strategy for evoking topographical or architectural details. When you are in the field, consider how your fieldsite differs from your surroundings at home. Although the differences will be more pronounced if you are abroad, there are plenty of regional or neighborhood variations within your home country. Describing urban spaces, rural downtowns, or gated suburban communities provides readers with essential socio-economic information about the world where your informants live.

For instance, I lived in California until my thirties. When I moved to Maine in 2002, everything about New England felt foreign to me: the cape-style houses with wooden clapboards and shakes, the rocky beaches, the narrow highways, the spectacular autumns, and the brutal winters. I grew up in southern California where droughts and wild fires rendered wooden houses impractical, where we had wide sandy beaches, massive six lane freeways, and few deciduous trees that lost their leaves. I never knew the difference between "annual" and "perennial" plants because almost everything was "perennial" in San Diego. Being "from away" (as they say in Maine) gave me a relative vocabulary with which to describe the Down East landscape.

In my first book, *The Red Riviera*, I wanted to start the introduction with a description of the Bulgarian Black Sea. Most of my readers had no idea that Bulgaria had beaches, let alone huge resort complexes. In the first two paragraphs, I evoked the Bulgarian seaside by filling the place with people and comparing the Black Sea coast to other, more familiar beach resorts:

> The sea breeze is salty and cooling. The operatic calls of the young men selling corn on the cob accompany the gruff hums of jet skis and the percussive gushing and smashing of the Black Sea. Topless Western European girls lounge beside portly Russian grandmothers. Wild gangs of preteen boys overrun the shoreline, dribbling soccer balls through the sand castles built by naked squealing toddlers. There are more than five thousand people enjoying the glorious day on the narrow band of beach in the resort of Albena.
>
> The fine sands on the shore are similar to the soft, pale grains in Koh Samui or Antigua. But compared to the lush, tropical ambience of Thailand or the Caribbean, Bulgaria feels distinctly European. There are no palm trees, no thatched huts, and the local peddlers threading their way through the sun-worshipping tourists are paler-skinned and carefully covered with thick, white smears of waterproof sunscreen. Looking out toward the sea, you see the usual array of water-sport equipment found at any major beach resort—paragliders, water skis, and paddle boats. This could be Greece, Italy,

or France, but a glance inland at the towering, cement hotels—
monolithic pillars of totalitarian architecture—betrays the landscape's communist past.[2]

In these opening paragraphs I started with the stereotypes of exotic
beaches: the Caribbean and Thailand. I conjured white sands, palm
trees, and shorelines crowded with tourists. Once the reader is thinking about beaches, I nudge their imaginations toward the slightly
more familiar European beaches of Greece or Southern France. Only
when I conjured the southern European seaside in the reader's mind
do I introduce the towering cement hotels that are distinct to the
Bulgarian resort of Albena. Even if you must rely on stereotypes, it
proves easier to evoke places when you provide a familiar referent.

You can also think about place as a metaphor for your social analysis. If one lawn grows wild in a neighborhood of immaculately land-
scaped front yards, highlight the contrast. Describe the social relevance of home garden care in this community, and what it means
when one family has given up. The visual of the one untended lawn
insinuates the creeping decimation of the American middle class.
The favelas above the beaches of Ipanema in Rio de Janeiro provide
another spatial contradiction that speaks volumes about wealth inequality in Brazil. The physical differences between neighborhoods
in Washington, DC, expose underlying socioeconomic realities—
for instance, the concentration of liquor stores and pawn shops in
poorer areas. As an ethnographer, think about how your description
of place can support your project's larger theoretical insights.

TELLING HISTORIES OF PLACE

All places have histories. Find out what was there before and how it
has changed over time. You can discuss the genealogy of a family by
talking about the history of their home. You can explore the process
of urbanization by describing the physical development of roads,
bridges, office parks, or malls. There are residential neighborhoods
in Thessaloniki, Greece, where apartment blocs rise up and surround

archeological sites that are millennia old. Modern Greeks confront the evidence of their long history in a way that few Americans can understand. City centers often contain the remnants of their past incarnations, and the thick description of these remains provides a vocabulary to explore what came before.

Evoke imagery to describe how spaces change and how those changes affect your informants. In the second chapter of *In Search of Respect*, Philippe Bourgois writes a street history of El Barrio, exploring Puerto Rico's colonial past, the Great Migration, the deindustrialization of New York and the loss of blue-collar jobs, and the contemporary political economy of New York City. Bourgois embeds this nuanced historical narrative in a textured physical description of East Harlem, which adds depth and tactility to the tale of Puerto Rican marginalization.

Another example comes from Elijah Anderson's *Code of the Street: Decency, Violence, and the Moral Life of the Inner City*. The introductory chapter of the book gives a panoramic view of social relations between blacks and whites in urban Philadelphia by exploring the various neighborhoods along Germantown Avenue. Anderson writes:

> Germantown Avenue is a major Philadelphia artery that dates back to colonial days. Eight and a half miles long and running mostly southeast, it links the northwest suburbs with the heart of inner-city Philadelphia. It traverses a varied social terrain as well. Germantown Avenue provides an excellent cross-section of the social ecology of a major American city. Along this artery live the well-to-do, the middle classes, the working poor, and the very poor—the diverse segments of urban society. The story of Germantown Avenue can therefore serve in many respects as a metaphor for the whole city.[3]

The discussion of the boutique stores, manicured parks, billboards, graffiti, empty lots, and boarded-up buildings as you progress down Germantown Avenue allow the reader to see and feel how social inequality in the United States manifests itself on the level of ordinary experience. From Chestnut Hill to Mount Airy to Germantown to the North Philadelphia ghetto, Anderson uses the physical description of the place to tell us a story about urban poverty that explodes with sensory information.

When I conducted my fieldwork in the deindustrializing city of Madan near the Bulgarian-Greek frontier, I spent a lot of time at an old soccer stadium. Under communism the local lead-zinc mining enterprise (GORUBSO) had a soccer team that competed with the soccer teams of other communist enterprises around Bulgaria. GORUBSO built the soccer stadium on the outskirts of Madan, and it became a vibrant center of community activity throughout the communist era. When I arrived in 2005, the stadium had fallen into disrepair. Local shepherds grazed their herds on the long grass. Occasionally, the local youth soccer team played a match on the pitch, but the bleachers and the team dressing rooms were crumbling into ruins. Unemployment spread like cancer, and youth fled the city in droves. The European Union promised funds to "beautify" Bulgaria, and in 2007 local residents successfully lobbied for their soccer stadium to be reconstructed using EU money. The stadium became a beacon of hope, a container for the dream that the EU could save the community from economic marginalization.

The history of the soccer stadium could operate as a metaphor for the volatile history of the city. Communism brought wealth and community. The postcommunist era (wherein GORUBSO was driven into bankruptcy) brought poverty and social dislocation. Madan residents pinned their hopes on Bulgaria's accession to the European Union on January 1, 2007, believing that Europe would provide jobs, bring their children home, and rebuild their community. In addition to giving the reader a visual sense of the foothills of the central Rhodopi Mountains, descriptions of the changing soccer stadium could represent the changing fortunes of the city.

In your own fieldwork, consider finding a street, bar, restaurant, business, or school. Investigate its history within the community you are studying. How might you expose its past through this particular place? How do the changes in this place represent larger transformations in the community?

Anthropologist Elizabeth Dunn conjures for the reader an American-style restaurant in Poland by filling it with people and their actions:

> The Falcon Inn offered high prices, foods fried in no-cholesterol vegetable oil, and tall blonde waitresses in T-shirts and short, cut-off jeans. It was rumored to be where the American businessmen went to eat. But on the Saturday night I was there, no American businessmen were to be seen. It was about eleven-thirty at night, certainly outside of regular business hours. As I sat on the sidewalk terrace, waiting for my drink, a group of Polish men arrived. They seated themselves at a café table. Then each one bent over, rummaged in his briefcase, and took out a cellular telephone. Carefully—almost reverently—each man placed his phone upright against the umbrella pole in the center of the table, so that the phones made a circle. None of the phones rang while the men were at the table, and none of the men made any calls.[4]

This short passage communicates the significance of The Falcon Inn for Polish men aspiring to be Western businessmen, performing an ideal of professionalism they associate with the introduction of capitalism in their country after 1989. The tall blonde waitresses in cut-off shorts, the Polish patrons with their non-ringing mobile phones, and the absent Americans all combine to tell a story about the importance of the restaurant as a theatre for acting out neoliberal dreams.

In ethnography, places often have relevance because of the actions performed by the people within them. One obvious way to bring a place to life is to populate it with your "characters" as Dunn has done above. Don't just write that there are children on a playground. Explain that there is a five-year-old girl pushing a younger boy on a dilapidated swing set. Don't just describe the village square as the social center of the community; show the people walking in and out of the post office and chatting at the outdoor tables of the café. Imagine the difference between a small town soccer stadium populated by shepherds and goats and that same stadium overflowing with cheering fans. The latter conjures up a vibrant and thriving local community whereas the former intimates that the population that once filled the soccer stadium has long gone.

Discussing the political economy of goods provides another avenue to enrich a manuscript with ethnographic details. Artifacts have politics, and most things exist within commodity chains. For example, sociologist and ethnographic filmmaker David Redmon conducted a multi-sited study of Mardi Gras beads in his book, *Bodies, Beads, and Trash*. Redmon moves from an examination of the social meaning of beads in New Orleans to the working conditions of the laborers who manufacture them overseas. These innocuous plastic strands link people together across time and space, and Redmon weaves a critical tale about globalization through a thoughtful focus on how individual lives are constrained by the politics of the nation-state where they are born. Commodities link people, places, practices, and beliefs.

Take careful notes and also describe the things that inhabit a space. Details about physical objects provide insight into the personalities of your informants. Once again, remember Sherlock Holmes's uncanny ability to deduce information about people by studying their possessions. When I am invited to someone's home, I always notice their books: how many there are and of what kind. I grew up in a household almost devoid of books, and I envied friends whose parents had personal libraries. In my 20s, I lived in the UK, Ghana, and Japan, and I learned how book ownership operated as a class marker across cultures. The more working class the family, the fewer the number of books, a consistent pattern I noticed in capitalist countries. One of the goals of the communists in Bulgaria, however, was to ensure that all citizens had books to read, and architects designed flats with prominent bookshelves. Miners and seamstresses built their own libraries, and for a while reading ceased to be an elite pastime. After 1989, the transition to capitalism once again commodified science and literature; private libraries regained their status as a privilege of a certain social class. Inanimate objects serve as invaluable rhetorical devices, especially when they contribute to the thick descriptions of rituals or events.

Describing Events

In the 1950s, W. Lloyd Warner and a team of researchers descended on the city of Newburyport, Massachusetts, as its citizens prepared for its 300th anniversary. Like Geertz's description of the Balinese cockfight, Warner's careful study of the parade allowed him to expound on "the symbolic life of the Americas."[5] Warner dissects the event of the tercentenary procession, and each of the individual floats, to tell a story of social stratification and class impermeability. Ethnographic details overflow, and the books provide another example of how thick description of a public event can be used as a window into the inner life of a community.

Events occur in successive steps through a finite period of time, and chronicling happenings can feel tedious. Practice recording details about events, even the most banal. Shortcuts will tempt you, but try to capture as much information as possible. When you sit down to describe the event in your final ethnographic text, the minute details form the backbone of your recounting, especially if the event or ritual serves as the basis for later interpretive analysis, such as Geertz's Balinese cockfight or Warner's tercentenary parade in Newburyport.

Challenge yourself with writing exercises. Get in an elevator and describe everything that happens as you travel from the ground floor to your destination. Observe each action you make and the actions of others sharing the elevator with you. Who presses the buttons? Where do people rest their eyes? Is anyone chatting? Is there someone constantly pressing the "close door" button at each level to try to speed the ascent? Is there someone who always places her arm out to hold the door for passengers running to get on? If you wanted to do an ethnomethodological experiment, ride the elevator with your back facing the door. Describe the way people react. Riding an elevator may lack deep cultural significance, but writing about elevator rides can help you hone your ability to chronicle events.

When writing about happenings, also consider how people relate to time. Is time something considered scarce or abundant? Do people wear wristwatches, and, if so, how often do they check them? How ubiquitous are clocks? Since most rituals, festivals, traditional events, and holidays happen at specific times (of the day, week, season, or year), frame these events within the wider cultural conception of time. Use events to explore your informants' particular relationship with time and how local histories, geographies, and social expectations shape this relationship. During the year I spent as a student at the University of Legon in Ghana, I noticed a relative absence of clocks and watches. Ghanaians obsessed less about time in general, but Accra also lies close enough to the equator that the sun rose and set at almost the same time throughout the year. The position of the sun told you everything you needed to know about the time. In Japan, on the other hand, clocks infest life. Japanese people rush about, and *"Jikan ga nai"* (There is no time) ranked among the first Japanese phrases I learned. In Bulgaria, time tortures the unemployed and retired who long for the jobs and security once guaranteed by the socialist state. In southern Germany (where I was living when I wrote this book), I heard church bells chime every fifteen minutes, and every hour gongs out across the town. I heard the time as often as I saw it, and Germans place great social value on punctuality.

Ethnographic texts come to life if they are rich with details about people, places, and events. Different strategies exist for writing about each of these categories, and ethnographers develop their own preferences and unique styles of thick description. Some ethnographers foreground specificities about people while others concentrate on places or use events as foundations for their interpretive insights. Details fuel social analysis in ethnography, and it is to this question of how to mix theory and thick description that we now turn.

CHAPTER 5

Integrate Your Theory

Every ethnographer must consider the balance between theory and data. Our fieldwork and our specific case studies render our work original, but this work fails to be scholarly if it lacks dialogue with larger theoretical concerns. When writing a dissertation, the literature review section remains de rigueur, but if the work is to be revised into a book, most acquisitions editors demand that this section be exorcised. If you are planning a series of articles, you will also need to trim the literature review into more manageable chunks to remain in accord with defined word counts. Weave the theoretical insights inspired by your participant observation into the final text. Share your original ideas without burying the reader under an avalanche of information about what other scholars, studying other cases, have said before you.

The task of integrating theory proves difficult for even the most experienced ethnographers, and different scholars maintain varying opinions on its importance. Some ethnographers put theory first, choosing a fieldwork site that will test the theory or fill a gap in the literature. Other ethnographers consider theory a secondary concern. They go to the field and allow the theory to emerge from the questions generated by their observations. Another subset of ethnographers might dispense with explicit theory altogether. Theoretical concerns dominated my early books and articles, but my more recent work places greater emphasis on the experience of everyday life. Theoretical inquiries underpin all of my research, but somewhere along the way I tired of foregrounding these questions.

Anthropologist John Borneman, the author of five ethnographic books, including the previously mentioned *Syrian Episodes*, has varied his scholarly style over the course of his career. He explained that:

> Theory always determines what I might write down [and] therefore preselects the data. But the theory of ethnography I hold to admonishes me to be open to encounters with the unexpected, to experience as much as possible, to allow myself to be subject to other people's desires and wishes as much as possible. But I go to the field with questions of larger social significance. What is the sacred? What is the political? What does it mean to be such and such a person at this time in such and such a place? I write down as much as I can in notes. I do not apply theory to this data but try to think through the data to refine, or even refute and displace, the questions I entered with.[1]

For Borneman, theory informs the questions that he brings to the field, but he does not allow the theory to infiltrate his fieldnotes. Instead, he places a heavy emphasis on participant observation, using his own experiences to question or subvert preconceived theoretical frameworks.

Amy Borovoy, an anthropologist and the author of *The Too-Good Wife: Alcohol, Codependency, and the Politics of Nurturance in Postwar Japan*, sees a more dialectic relationship between data and theory in her own work. She writes:

> I'm tempted to say the data are more important, but that's not right, because one needs ideas to interpret and organize the data. However if one simply demonstrates the same ideas (Foucault's ideas about biopolitics [for instance]) in many different field settings, it's no longer interesting. [Theory and data] shape each other in a fluid way. One starts with theoretical ideas or questions that come from theoretical readings, historical data, or other ethnographies. Then one's ethnographic findings shape those questions.[2]

Like Borneman, Borovoy values theory as part of the road map that guides the initial fieldwork. But once again, theory is a necessary, but not sufficient, ingredient for a successful ethnography. The data from the field leads the analysis and eventual writing of ethnographic texts, and one has to be careful not to reproduce studies that have already been conducted in other contexts, providing just one more data point for an already well-established theory.

Some ethnographers place more emphasis on the value of ethnographic data as a story one tells about the field. Julie Hemment, an anthropologist and the author of *Empowering Women in Russia*, also believes that theory determines the questions that shape her fieldwork. When it comes to writing, however, she prefers the richness of ethnographic detail. She writes:

> I'd say [theory and data] are equally important, and totally shot through with one another. While I consider myself to be led by my ethnographic data, it's theory that has shaped its collection. And in analyzing, I tack back and forth between them continually. As far as what makes it onto the page—my personal preference as a reader and writer is for theoretically informed ethnographically rich texts and so I try to avoid theory-laden digressions. And nothing grabs a reader like a good story.[3]

Some colleagues in sociology also tend to place a heavier emphasis on their ethnographic data. Olga Shevchenko, author of *Crisis and the Everyday in Postsocialist Moscow*, explains, "I love theory as much as the next gal, but in the end, its role for me is to illuminate life, and so for me, ethnographic details come first."[4] When I asked David Redmon, author of *Bodies, Beads, and Trash: Public Sex, Global Labor, and the Disposability of Mardi Gras*, how he found a balance between theory and data, he said that he took his cues from his editor, who encouraged him to write his book "in filmic ways." Redmon also relied on friendly readers. He sent rough drafts of his manuscript to colleagues, and "every person responded to the experiential material more . . . than the theoretical analysis." In response to this feedback, Redmon let the stories lead the narrative and only added in brief theoretical discussions at the end of each chapter.

The key to writing a readable ethnography lies within the ability to interweave the necessary theory into the ethnographic article, report, dissertation, or book without overloading the reader with extraneous verbiage. Beginning ethnographers sometimes bracket out their ethnographic data into separate chapters or textual interludes. For instance, Anne Allison's 1994 book, *Nightwork: Sexuality, Pleasure, and Corporate Masculinity in a Tokyo Hostess Club*, dedicates the first third of her text to a thick description of an exclusive bar catering to Japanese "salarymen." This opening section entices the reader to Japan and gives a visceral sense of participation in the Japanese nightlife industry. The second part of the book contains a literature review and some historical background. Allison provides her theoretical and interpretive analysis in the final third. Although the structure works, the book feels oddly disjointed at times, as if she took three long papers and pasted them together. The first section establishes her authority as a participant observer and her considerable talent as a writer, but the rest of the book seems like excerpts from a dissertation.

I have taught *Nightwork* in my senior seminars for over ten years, and in each course my undergraduate students comment on the stark difference between the three sections. Allison did revise her dissertation into the book *Nightwork*, and as I said earlier, dissertations are credentialing exercises, and the best dissertation is a done dissertation. As far as revised dissertations go, *Nightwork* excels at capturing the imagination of the reader and letting the data lead the theory, but as a book, it would hold together better if Allison slipped more of the history and theory in amongst the thick description.

Sociologist Katja Guenther's 2010 book, *Making Their Place: Feminism after Socialism in Eastern Germany*, presents a different model. Guenther includes ethnographic interludes between her analytical chapters. These interludes are sprinkled throughout the book, and they return the reader to the people and places of the former German Democratic Republic. I used a similar device when revising my own dissertation. I told one young woman's personal story over the course of the manuscript by interspersing little ethnographic vignettes about her preparations for a university entrance exam between chapters. In the conclusion, I intertwined the story of Svetla with my broader theoretical arguments, bringing the narrative and the theoretical analysis together at the close. The ethnographic interlude provides a middle ground between a separate theory/literature review section and the total integration of this material into your ethnographic data. You can include passages of thick description without editing them into the more analytical parts of the text. If you are under time pressure, write up specific scenes and insert them between your chapters to give the book a little more narrative flow.

For some books, you may have ethnographic interludes and analytical chapters in combination with some fully integrated chapters. The anthropologist Gerald Creed starts his book *Masquerade and Postsocialism* with one analytic introductory chapter and then follows this with a purely descriptive second chapter. The rest of his book, however, provides a great example of a senior anthropologist weaving his ethnographic material into his critical analysis. Chapter three is an exceptional piece of readable ethnography with Creed moving back and forth between scenes of ritual mumming in Bulgaria and rich theoretical insights about gender, using descriptions of village performances to explore shifting definitions of masculinity.

Another example of the interweaving of theory and data comes from the sociologist Jessica Fields. In her 2008 book, *Risky Lessons: Sex Education and Social Inequality*, Fields uses the first person to narrate her own understanding of how theory informs her data. Fields did research in three North Carolina middle schools to explore how different sex education programs reinforce gender, race, and class inequalities. She opens one chapter with her own memory of a feminist theory seminar that she took in the late 1990s at the University of North Carolina. Fields recounts how one woman in her class was surprised to learn that her son, an eighth grader, learned about clitoral and vaginal orgasms in his sex education class at school.

The other graduate students, mostly women, also felt disturbed. A second student asked what they found so dangerous about this information, wondering when it was appropriate for young people to be taught about female pleasure rather than just about pregnancy avoidance and sexually transmitted diseases. Reflecting on the memory, Fields writes:

> The pleasures and dangers of sexual expression and knowledge lie at the heart of this chapter. Having thought for years about sex education, I find myself slightly embarrassed by my initial reaction to the prospect of students learning in a middle school sex education classroom about clitoral orgasms. I recognize the heteronormativity of the concerns we expressed in the seminar: we placed boys and girls in a seemingly inevitable and antagonistic relationship with each other, and we failed to consider that girls might also learn how they might participate in their own and others' clitoral orgasms. I feel impatient with my worry that learning about sexual pleasure would compromise eighth graders' sexual innocence, as if young people are not always and already navigating a sexual world rife with conflicting and confusing sexual messages.[5]

Fields uses this passage to introduce a long discussion about the theories surrounding the supposed danger of female sexuality and the difficulties teachers face when discussing sexual pleasure in public schools. The discussion grows naturally from her field observations and personal experiences rather than being an exercise in scholarly erudition for its own sake.

Perhaps the extreme case of integrating your theory is to exclude it. Another curiosity of John Borneman's *Syrian Episodes* is that it stretches the limits of the ethnographic form. In addition to putting himself fully into his ethnography, he also includes no explicit theoretical discussions or literature reviews and favors a final bibliographic essay over citations in the text. In this book, Borneman encourages ethnographers to get back into the field and make face-to-face contact with real people in foreign cultures despite the uncomfortable power imbalances this entails. Borneman fears that the demands of theoretical argumentation stifle the potential insights made possible by sustained observation. He writes:

> I have come to think that the quality of writing as well as our interpretative skills has been compromised by subsuming all listening, viewing, observation, interaction, comparison, and contextualization into historical narratives. Lost is the accidental, incidental, and occasional; the serendipitous, fateful and irregular; events and scenes that don't always hang together, that resist facile inclusion in a temporal development or argument. Lost is the episodic: experience that is personal, tied to a particular time and place, a part that does not readily fit into the whole.[6]

Of course, some might argue that these rhetorical opportunities exist only for the tenured elite. Junior scholars need to strut their theoretical stuff in their first articles and books. Academia possesses a guild mentality. New members gain admittance by paying due homage to the ideas and publications of their scholarly elders. Citations and literature reviews provide a forum for recognizing the contributions of those who came before you, and woe unto the researcher who sends an article out to a peer-reviewed journal without citing the work of one of the peer reviewers. Since the process is blind, the reports could come from anyone in your field. To reference all work even tangentially related to your own makes sense in this context.

Recent studies expose how senior professionals haze their junior peers to ensure citation. In a 2008 working paper for the National Bureau of Economic Research, Joshua Aizenman and Kenneth Kletzer identified what they called the "citation death tax" for scholars and papers in economics. The authors used a sample of 428 papers written by 16 well-known economists who, for a variety of reasons, died significantly before the age of retirement. For about half of the scholars in this sample, there was a huge drop in the number of citations of their work after their death. Aizenman and Kletzer argue that since citation rates form a proxy measure for the importance of scholarly

work, and universities use citation rates to determine merit increases
in salary, "authors have a pecuniary incentive to promote citation of
their work."[7] By identifying the post-death drop off in citation rates,
Aizenman and Kletzer claim that roughly half of senior scholars use
their influence to ensure that colleagues cite their work.

In other words, extended literature reviews and long theoretical
discussions provide an avenue for junior scholars wishing to avoid the
wrath of the uncited. Once a senior scholar loses the ability to influence the career of other researchers, citation rates plummet. Junior
scholars no longer fear the consequences of an omission. In ethnography, the length and comprehensiveness of your literature review,
as well as the extent of your theoretical analysis, may be influenced
by the specter of senior colleagues rejecting a book or article manuscript out of spite. As a writer, you should be cognizant of your own
motivations. Let yourself be guided by reasonable judgment. While
an egregious omission can spell doom for a manuscript, generous
anonymous reviewers can recommend a "revise and resubmit" and
suggest a list of references for you to include with your revision.

So how do you decide how much theoretical analysis to include,
and how can you integrate it into your data so that it does not seem
like theoretical analysis for its own sake? Once again different ethnographers work with their fieldnotes in varying ways. Olga Shevchenko
struggles to decide what parts of her fieldnotes to include:

> I almost never know in advance which parts of the field notes will go
> into the text, because it takes me some time, and a lot of writing, to
> figure out what it is exactly that I am going to argue! With interviews,
> it's different. There are some turns of phrase that seem to leap off the
> page, and these are usually those that capture experience in a fresh or
> complex way. I also tend to notice when a turn of phrase, or a meta-
> phor emerges more than once. When I heard a third person compare
> their everyday life with living on a volcano, I knew it was going to be
> in the book in a major way. But it also got me thinking to what this
> metaphor accomplished, which sent me right back to the field notes.

When I can't find a place in the text for an evocative image or turn of phrase that I hear from a respondent, this causes me great torments![8]

Olga's process mirrors my more recent modus operandi. I spend a lot of time reading my fieldnotes and deciding what material I want to include before I figure out my core argument, a process sometimes called "grounded theory," a way of incorporating theoretical insights that emerge from the fieldwork, rather than letting theoretical questions guide it. Like Olga, I look out for great quotes or turns of phrase that capture something about the everyday experience of my informants. Julie Hemment also allows recollections of fieldwork to guide her writing:

> My first step is to recall a rich incident. Often it's an interaction or an event that played out in ways I didn't fully understand at the time — something that snagged my attention and caused me to linger, and maybe something that I continue to puzzle. I then return to my fieldnotes for more texture (and these places, incidents, moments are often places where I did write thickly to begin with). The ethnographic writing I ultimately produce is an amalgam of all this. I rarely incorporate my fieldnotes directly, or quote from them; rather, I write from them.[9]

If you are the kind of ethnographer who starts with the stories and writes her way into a theoretical insight, write out your thick descriptions first, but then take care not to overload the reader with a wall of theoretical analysis at the end of the book. Once you have completed your first draft, work back into the manuscript and foreshadow your theoretical argument throughout the body of your text. If done with a light hand these insertions will not break the flow of your narrative, but will gently guide the reader to your ultimate conclusions.

Other anthropologists know their conclusions before they begin. When I wrote my dissertation, theoretical interventions guided my writing from page one. I knew from the outset that I wanted to argue

against a Western feminist consensus which declared that East European women would be negatively affected by the collapse of communism and the introduction of free markets. If you are starting with a
clear argument, examine your fieldnotes. Identify the ethnographic
material that will best substantiate your claims. Then, state your overall theoretical intervention in the introduction to the article or book.
Make this a brief statement without too many rhetorical flourishes
and without the exhaustive literature review. As you write up the relevant examples from your fieldwork, occasionally stop and return to
your argument and theoretical framework, inserting bits of theoretical background among the ethnographic examples. Sprinkle
these theoretical asides throughout your text, ensuring they complement the anecdotes you have chosen.

Anthropologist Doug Rogers somehow manages to use these two
strategies at the same time:

> Whatever balance I'm aiming for with a particular piece of writ-
> ing, I'm generally sorting secondary literature right along with the
> fieldnotes and other sources. So I might have a section of my book-
> shelves labeled "Chapter 2," a folder of academic articles on the com-
> puter named "Chapter 2," and another folder of fieldnotes and other
> sources (newspapers, archival materials, whatever) also labeled chap-
> ter 2. When I'm working on chapter 2, I'm trying to keep all of these
> things in play, and the "theory" stuff gets sorted and resorted right
> along with the fieldnotes as I write and reclassify, write and reclassify.
> For this last book, one way I did this was by covering my wall with
> sticky notes that indicated chapter sections and subsections and the
> bits of ethnography and/or theory that would go in each . . . that way
> I could move things around easily. I would write and keep looking
> back and forth between the sticky notes and the other things labeled
> chapter 2 — notes, articles, books, etc.[10]

You can write up your data and then add in your theory, or you
can start with your theory and slip in your data, or if you can manage it, try to do both at the same time. Whatever your method, avoid

separate sections or chapters devoted solely to literature review and
theoretical analysis at the beginning of your text. Also, be honest
with yourself and excise any extraneous discussions that exist merely
to avoid the displeasure of a senior colleague. If displeasure is foresee-
able, dump those discussions into a substantive endnote.

Of course there will always be exceptions to these guidelines—
some journals may require a separate literature review section, others
may prefer publishing heavy theoretical analysis only lightly sea-
soned with ethnographic examples. Every situation is unique, but
in general, a readable ethnography prioritizes thick ethnographic detail over long-winded theoretical analysis, and integrates that theory
into the narrative flow of the text.

CHAPTER 6

Embrace Dialogue

"I think this part of the chapter would be stronger if you broke up some of these quotes and wrote them as dialogue," the professor said.

The student crossed her arms. "But most ethnographies use block quotes or straight transcriptions. I want to be faithful to the original conversation."

"Writing good dialogue can be more faithful, because you can include specific details about vocal intonations and body language."

"But I don't know how to write dialogue." The student frowned.

"Pick up some of your favorite ethnographies, and see if you can emulate the style. Try to liven up this material a bit."

The student took the draft chapter and squinted at the notes in the margins of his pages. "Okay. I'll give it a shot."

Dialogue brings a manuscript to life, allowing your informants to speak directly to the reader, but disciplinary conventions constrain its use. In *Writing Ethnographic Fieldnotes*, Emerson, Fretz, and Shaw explain that there are three ways to include voices from the field: through direct and indirect quotation, through reported speech, and through paraphrasing. They argue that only direct quotes from your informants should be placed within quotation marks and therefore presented as "authentic" dialogue. Anything that falls outside of "authentic" dialogue must be reported or paraphrased.

But what counts as "authentic" depends on a variety of other factors: the nature of your fieldwork, whether you record or take notes, and the native language of your informants. If you record English-speaking informants you can excerpt long passages of their conversations from your transcriptions onto the page. As an ethnographer, you frame these excerpts, putting them in the proper context. Once contextualized, these excerpts serve as the raw data for your subsequent scholarly analysis. Be careful, however, not to overload your reader with lengthy block quotations that break the flow of your narrative. Even if you have perfect transcriptions of your informants' words, be sure to mix in some paraphrasing with direct quotation. In Esther Newton's classic book, *Mother Camp*, one whole chapter contains the direct transcriptions of several female impersonator acts, and my students never fail to complain about how tedious it is to read pages of pure monologue. Verbatim dialogue can be artfully crafted to engage your reader.

Philippe Bourgois's *In Search of Respect* provides a great example of the verbatim approach. Bourgois used a tape recorder in the field and includes long quoted passages from Primo and Cesar (his two primary informants), preserving the rhythm and cadence of their speech as well as their slang and idiomatic expressions. Bourgois gives the reader "stage directions" as bracketed parentheticals to fill in for the nonverbal cues that the reader will not get from the text alone. Bourgois tells us when people are [interrupting], [ignoring], [laughing], or [imitating a high-pitched whine], as well as when there are [gunshots] or [more gunshots]. By using these cues, Bourgois brings these transcriptions to life, which makes for compelling reading.

The verbatim approach proves difficult when you are dealing with a foreign language not easily translated into English. When I write fieldnotes, I produce them in what I call "Bunglish," a mixture of Bulgarian and English. I listen to speech while making note of body language, tone of voice, and the movements of eyes as people talk. In Bulgaria, I feel uncomfortable using a tape recorder; many Bulgarians, especially those raised under communism, associate tape recorders with duplicitous journalists or the secret police. People relax with me when I take notes by hand in a simple school notebook without a machine recording words that can later be played back and perhaps used against them. I also write more detailed notes when I know I have no backup. If I jot down a good quote or anecdote, I repeat back what has been said in Bulgarian to ensure that I have captured their correct meaning. Then it's my job to render the quote into colloquial English.

On the few occasions I have used recording devices in Bulgaria (with the permission of my interviewees), I consider presenting quotes in the original Bulgarian and then providing English translations in parentheses, like so:

> "Не съм християнин. Не съм мюсюлманин. Аз съм атеист." [*I am not a Christian. I am not a Muslim. I am an atheist.*]
>
> "Вие сте марксист." [*You are a Marxist.*]
>
> "Точен марксист. Моята философия е проста. Винаги десният крак напред, когато излизате от дома си. От дясната страна е живот и доброта, а от ляво е смъртта и всичко, което е лошо." [*An exact Marxist. My philosophy is simple. Always the right foot forward when you leave the house. On the right side is life and goodness, and on the left is death and everything that is bad.*]

But few readers can decipher Cyrillic, and the repetition of the same quote adds words to a manuscript. When I struggle against upper word limits, I cut the Bulgarian quotes before anything else.

To approximate this purist style, some anthropologists working in foreign languages present block quotes in English but include selected parentheticals of the original language, transliterated into Latin letters. Examples of this style can be found in Amy Borovoy's *The Too-Good Wife* and Saba Mahmood's *Politics of Piety: The Islamic Revival and the Feminist Subject*, an ethnography about women in Egypt. In both cases, the ethnographers use a mixture of direct quotations and block quotes with transliterations of the original Japanese or Arabic appearing next to some (but not all) sentences. While this does gesture to the authenticity of the quotes, and demonstrates the foreign language mastery of the authors, the parentheticals provide little benefit to the reader unless she speaks Japanese or Arabic.

And if the authors expect readers to know Japanese or Arabic, why transliterate the foreign language quotes into Latin letters? It also proves difficult to decipher why foreign language parentheticals accompany some quotes, but not others. Are these quotes and phrases highlighted for special attention? In some cases, you use foreign language parentheticals when there are multiple possible translations for a word or phrase. In my own writing, I have also included English translations of Bulgarian quotes accompanied by parentheticals of the original Bulgarian words transliterated from the Cyrillic into the Latin alphabet. For instance:

> "An exact Marxist (*tochen Marksist*)," he added. "My philosophy is simple (*Moyata filosofiya e prosta*). Always the right foot forward when you leave the house. On the right side is life and goodness, and on the left is death and everything that is bad."

The Bulgarian word "*tochen*" can mean "exact," "precise," or "accurate," and my informant was using it to highlight his embrace of what he believed to be orthodox Marxism. This parenthetical denoted a possible conflict of interpretations. But other parentheticals were just direct translations. I included many of these in *Muslim Lives in Eastern Europe*, and my copyeditor at Princeton University Press called me out on it. She asked me why I was seasoning my paragraphs and quotations with random Bulgarian words. At that time, I remember thinking: "Isn't that what I am supposed to do?" I internalized a disciplinary convention and included parentheticals because that's what other anthropologists did. I also liked the way they looked. I told none of this to the copyeditor.

Instead, I explained that I wanted to remind the reader that the conversations in my book happened in Bulgarian, and that the parentheticals provided a flavor of a language most English-speaking readers had never heard. I insisted on keeping my Bulgarian words and phrases, but I relented on the full sentences in Bulgarian. The copyeditor argued that they added little to my argument and interrupted the narrative with text that most readers would skip anyway.

She relented in the end, but now I see that she was right. Foreign language parentheticals confuse nonexpert readers.

No matter how much you strive for purism in representation, your presence in the field influences both the production and recording of dialogue. As an ethnographer, you deploy your interpretive skills to render dialogue so that it best captures the cultural meaning and relevance of that dialogue to your informants. Translations from a foreign language can never be literal; they must channel the tone and spirit of the conversations you overheard. Even if you are working in English, walls of verbatim quotes will bore your reader unless they are broken up and properly contextualized. As long as you are absolutely faithful to the nature of those conversations, you can ethically render ethnographic dialogue using literary forms.

The anthropologist Paul Stoller writes brilliant ethnographic dialogue in his studies of the Songhay People of Niger. Stoller favors this literary approach, translating words into English and presenting them as direct quotations, without any burdensome parentheticals. Here is a scene from his 1989 book, *Fusion of the Worlds*:

The woman who had commissioned the dance approached Serci and Mahamane Sergu with her son, who would soon marry. They sat on the sand at the feet of the spirits, with the sorko who was to serve as the intermediary.

"What must I do to protect the marriage of my son?" the woman asked the sorko.

The sorko posed the same question to Serci:

"Sorko, tell the woman she must acquire one white chicken, one red chicken, and one speckled chicken. These she must kill and then give the cooked meat to the poor." Serci paused a moment. "Do you understand, sorko? Do you understand my message?"

"Yes, yes, my chief. I understand."

Serci continued. "Sorko. This young man must acquire the egg of a white hen. He must dig a hole under the acacia at the crossroads on the Mangezie Road—Sorko, do you hear my message?"

"I do, indeed, my chief."

"Sorko," Serci said, "if they follow my words the marriage will have peace and happiness only. Peace and happiness. Sorko, do you follow me?"

"I do, indeed, Serci." The sorko repeated the prescriptions to the mother and son.[1]

In this section of dialogue, Stoller provides a window into an every-day interaction between a spirit medium and those who come to seek advice. From the context Stoller sets for this scene, the reader knows that this conversation wasn't spoken in English. He interprets the dialogue he heard in the field, placing everything in direct quo-tation, temporarily removing himself from the scene, and giving the reader the sense of being there, in Niger, to overhear this conversa-tion. Stoller could have paraphrased this exchange, reporting the gist of the conversation and explaining its significance for his argument. But the dialogue brings life and narrative movement to what would otherwise be another solid paragraph of expository text.

Other fantastic examples of ethnographic dialogue can be found in anthropologist Alma Gottlieb and Philip Graham's co-authored book, *Parallel Worlds: An Anthropologist and a Writer Encounter Africa*, and from the sociologist Shamus Rahman Kahn in his book *Privilege: The Making of an Adolescent Elite at St. Paul's School*. Kahn was an assistant professor at Columbia University when he did the research for the book. He was an alumnus and returned to St. Paul's as a faculty member to do his participant observation among the students. In this short passage, he allows a snippet of dialogue to ex-plain the deep cynicism prevalent among elite prep school students:

Carla, a role model, took her position seriously and kept tabs on how new students were adjusting. "How'd you do on that paper?" she asked Lacy.

"I don't know. I feel like I totally bullshitted it."

Carla, emphasizing that that was not the question, replied, "Well? How'd you do?"

"Fine, I guess," Lacy said uncomfortably. "But it was weird."

Reassuring Lacy, but in a way that seemed to directly confront the core principles of the school, Carla told her, "Well, that's what you learn to do here. Bullshit your way through."[1]

In *Body and Soul*, Loïc Wacquant artfully incorporates the vernacular language of his African-American informants. Anthropologist Kirin Narayan celebrates narrative forms of ethnographic writing in her book, *Alive in the Writing: Crafting Ethnography in the Company of Chekhov*. This book contains a valuable section on "voice," which every aspiring ethnographer must read.

So how do you write good dialogue? First, comb through your fieldnotes and find sections where you have recorded full conversations. Alternatively, transcribe your interview recordings and look for long quotes or discussions that might create a dynamic scene. In general, passages of dialogue should provide a basis for later discussion, but you might also include some dialogue to set a scene or to familiarize the reader with your informants. Once you have found these passages, do your best to render the conversation as faithfully as you can to the original. Some ethnographers will include a footnote, endnote, or a paragraph in their preface or introduction, explaining how dialogue has been handled in their text—for instance, if only transcribed dialogue is in quotes. In this note, you can also discuss translation and transliteration issues, as well as explain who did those translations.

If you are working in English from a recording, transcribe the words but make note of natural pauses, laughter, changes in vocal tone, or interruptions. Try to fill in details about the setting of the conversation and include descriptions of body language (if you can remember them). Language has meaning in context, and you must provide a setting. If you have spent a lot of time with your informants, you should have memories of their facial expressions, gestures, and the cadence and variation of their voices. Incorporate this information into your passages of dialogue.

You can make room for these details by limiting the verbs you use when attributing quotes. Most writers prefer the word "said" over verbs like "exclaimed" or "asked" because they are redundant of punctuation. For instance, you don't need to use the verb "asked" if there is already a question mark at the end of the sentence.

"Do you want me to get you something?" I asked.

The "I asked" is already implied by the "do you" at the beginning of the sentence and by the question mark at the end. Compare these two sentences:

1. "You want me to get you something?"
2. "You want me to get you something."

The first is a question and the second is a statement. We know this from the punctuation. The same goes for the word "exclaimed."

"I hate you!" she exclaimed.

The statement "I hate you" and the exclamation point tell the reader that this is an exclamation. Much better to write:

"Do you want me to get you something from the store?" I said.
    "I hate you!" she said.
    She raised her voice and stamped her foot. "I hate you!"

Overuse of adverbs in dialogue attributions can make for weak writing: "she said proudly," "he said cheerfully," or "I said disapprovingly." Many adverbs used to describe character are a way of telling rather than showing, and as an ethnographer you should include as much detail about your informants as possible. "She said haughtily" can become "She lifted her chin and said . . ." "He said cheerfully" can become "He laughed and said . . ." "I said disapprovingly" can become "I crossed my arms over my chest, shook my head, and said . . ."

Body language and vocal inflection renders dialogue more realistic, which is why anthropologists like Philippe Bourgois feel compelled to insert details in brackets even when working with verbatim transcriptions. As you work with your own fieldnotes or transcriptions, always look for places where you can use specificities about your informants to portray them as real people and not merely as speakers of words that provide data for your subsequent analysis.

Dialogue also allows room for white space on a page. Academic books often contain long blocks of text, and dialogue creates visual variation. White space gives the eyes a rest, and you create this space by starting a new paragraph for each speaker (even if that speaker isn't speaking words). For instance:

> "I am going to the store," I said, poking my head into Desislava's room.
> Desislava nodded.
> "Do you want me to get you anything?"
> "No, thanks," Desislava said.

Body language can count as a form of dialogue, just as it does in real life. Desislava's nod serves as acknowledgement that she heard me. She spoke no words, but meaning was communicated.

You can also use body language to stand in for dialogue attribution, as in:

> "No thanks." Desislava shook her head. "I don't need anything right now."

Practice writing dialogue by listening to conversations and writing them out in dialogue form. Use "said" as much as possible and replace adverbs with descriptions of actions. Craft handbooks on writing dialogue abound, but you can also learn by reading ethnographies that use dialogue and emulating their style. If you combine dialogue with ethnographic details, the first person, and integrated theory, you are well on your way to writing an ethnography that can find an audience beyond your tight circle of scholarly peers.

CHAPTER 7

Include Images

Almost everyone knows this cliché: "a picture is worth a thousand words." Scholars have long attributed the origin of this quote to Frederick Barnard, an American adman, who published two variations of the quote in *Printer's Ink* in 1921 and 1927. The Yale Book of Quotations challenges this theory, claiming that a version of the phrase appeared in a real estate advertisement in the *New York Times* in 1914. The true origin of the sentiment probably dates back to the 1862 book *Fathers and Sons*. There, Ivan Turgenev wrote, "The drawing shows me at a glance what would be spread over ten pages in a book." Whatever its source, the phrase earned its cliché status because it's true.

Advertisers and journalists know the awesome power of the image and exploit it regularly. Economists and natural scientists employ charts and graphs to represent their findings, and quantitative social scientists use tables to summarize data. The qualitative nature of ethnographic data does not translate well into charts, graphs, or tables, and ethical concerns about maintaining the anonymity of our informants discourage the use of photographs that contain the faces of our research subjects. Despite these challenges, pictures from our fieldsites can and should be used to complement our thick descriptions.

Two strategies exist for including photographs into your ethnographic work. The first is photoethnography: a scholarly study that relies on images as much as it does on words to substantiate its arguments or expose the reader to a particular community. In anthropology, excellent examples include Philippe Bourgois's *Righteous Dope-fiend*, João Biehl's *Vita* and *Will to Live*, and Ruth Behar's *An Island Called Home*. All three authors collaborated with photographers to fill their pages with black and white images of men and women in the field. Sociology also overflows with examples of photoethnography. Mitchell Duneier's *Sidewalk* includes the professional photographs of Ovie Carter, a Pulitzer Prize–winning photographer for the *Chicago Tribune*. *Sidewalk* examines the lives of homeless men in Greenwich Village, and the stark photographs capture the everyday activities of African-American men subsisting on the streets of New York City in the 1990s. The chapter on the magazine vendors includes haunting images of men hawking discarded periodicals. The photographs complement the text, humanizing the men ignored by so many urban residents.

Douglas Harper embraced the roles of sociologist and photographer. His first book, *Good Company*, grew out of his dissertation research following homeless men (what he calls "tramps") across the country. The book provides another example of how photography can complement qualitative research. Harper's second book, *Working Knowledge*, used photographs to illustrate the lived experience of work, specifically of the manual skilled labor done by Willie, a "Jack-of-all trades" handyman. The close-up pictures capture the lost art of fixing things; we see hands hammering, welding, holding various bits of metal, tightening vices, drilling holes, filing, and otherwise handling power tools. One striking series of photographs celebrates the repair of a transmission. A series of nine images shows Willie's hands "removing the ring gear," "saving a gasket," and "getting inside the transmission."[1]

Loïc Wacquant's book *Body and Soul* incorporates the author's photographs in an unconventional way. Selected images are published with the original edges of the Kodak film roll framing them — black strips of negative with white rectangular film perforations. The photo numbers are stamped on the filmstrip near each image, as are the words "Kodak 5009" or "Kodalux Processing." The physicality of the film reminds the reader that there was someone, a sociologist, taking the pictures. These are not just images, but a diary of personal snapshots from the field.

Most of us lack the photographic skills to fill our pages with professional quality photos, nor do we have professional photographers willing to donate their images to our academic projects, for which they will receive little or no remuneration. Copyright law and strict permission regimes for photographs render it expensive to borrow images for your books or articles, a situation further exacerbated by the high cost of stock imagery from companies like Corbis or Getty Images. On the other hand, there exist an ever-increasing number of images freely available under "Creative Commons" licenses. The falling price of good digital cameras and smartphones means that even amateurs can capture quality images when they are in the field. And you can always consider the personal photo albums of your informants (as long as they give you permission).

For each of my four books I included an increasing number of images—from about ten photos in my first to fifty-seven in the most recent. For *The Red Riviera* I used a combination of photographs from an old point-and-shoot film camera and communist-era postcards that I bought from street vendors in Sofia. I developed my own photos commercially and sent the hard copies to Duke University Press for the creation of the black-and-white halftones. Academic presses demand that you have permissions for all of the images you wish to include. I learned from this initial experience that if I wanted to use images in my books, I should learn some photography.

When I began the fieldwork for my second project, I spent $400 to buy a decent digital camera with a small zoom lens. This was an early Panasonic Lumix with optical image stabilization for my shaky hands. Small enough to keep in a jacket pocket, the camera took photos with a high enough resolution to meet the standards required by most publishing houses (300 dpi). Over the year of my fieldwork, I snapped thousands of photos with that little camera. Legal regimes around photography vary from country to country, but in general pictures taken of any subject on public property become the property of the photographer (as are images taken of people on private property as long as the photographer was standing on public property—a loophole mightily abused by the zoom lens-wielding paparazzi of every nation). Photographers enjoy incredible copyright protections, and you have the right to publish almost any photograph you take. For close-ups, works of art or architecture, and photographs of sensitive activities or military installations, always ask permission before clicking the shutter (and be sure you don't need permissions before you publish).

From these thousands of images, I faced the torturous decision of which ones to include in the final book. Princeton University Press allowed me twenty-five images, so I had to choose the ones that best supported my analytical arguments. For *Muslim Lives in Eastern Europe*, I wanted to illustrate the difference between traditional Bulgarian Islamic dress and the new "orthodox" Islamic dress as well as the new variations of mosque architecture in the region. I explained these things in words, but the inclusion of photographs let me show the reader images of women dressed in different styles and of old and new mosques side by side. I also included historical images of Madan from the communist era beside my own photographs of Madan in 2005, a city crumbling into ruin. Those images supplemented my tale of the deindustrialization of the city after the collapse of communism.

A good image bolsters the content of your book; it helps tell your story. In *Blue-Chip Black*, sociologist Karyn Lacy includes photos of the luxurious suburban homes of the black middle class in Maryland—two car garages and careful landscaping that made them indistinguishable from the homes of their white middle-class peers. Even the simplest snapshot can enrich an ethnographic narrative, and I encourage all ethnographers to invest in a decent camera (or a good smartphone with a camera) before heading off into the field. Basic photo editing software comes preloaded on most computers and mobile devices, and free packages proliferate online. With this technology, you can zoom in, straighten, sharpen, or otherwise enhance your images (although some university presses prefer to receive the unedited original with instructions for manipulation).

Mosque 1—A new mosque built in the Rhodope Mountains after the collapse of communism in 1989. Photo by Kristen Ghodsee.

In *Lost in Transition*, I also included a combination of my own images with a collection of photos from the family albums of my Bulgarian friends and colleagues. Since the book discussed everyday life during and after communism, these photo albums seemed a natural place to go to collect images of ordinary people. I wanted to capture

Mosque 2—A traditional Bulgarian mosque in the same region. Photo by Kristen Ghodsee.

the normality of life before 1989, and I selected pictures of families at the seaside, of friends hanging out, of couples strolling, and of children smiling from the front of seasonal greeting cards. Since I could not take the originals, I used a portable flatbed scanner and scanned photos as high-resolution tiff files. These files required many gigabytes each, and I traveled with external hard drives to avoid overloading my laptop. Today, cloud computing makes digital storage even easier, as long as you take reasonable precautions about data security and make sure your files are password protected.

In each case, I typed up a short request for permission from the owners of the photographs, using some language borrowed from my press:

Dear X,

As the author of the forthcoming book tentatively titled *Lost in Transition: Ethnographies of Everyday Life after Communism*, I am responsible for clearing and paying for rights and permissions with the advice and support of the scholarly publisher Duke University Press. I would like to include in this book the following images, which belong to you:

1. Photo 1
2. Photo 2
3. Photo 3

To make this work easily available to scholars, I am requesting non-exclusive publishing rights for using the requested material in this book and in any excerpts of this book, regardless of the media, territories, and languages in which it is distributed and displayed.

I will acknowledge the source of your material in accordance with scholarly norms. If you require any particular form of acknowledgement, please let me know. If these terms are agreeable to you, please sign your name on the line below.

Sincerely,
Kristen

When I submitted my artwork to the press, I provided signed copies of these letters. They proved sufficient to reproduce the photos in the book.

In *Lost in Transition*, I included some of my own personal photos, a decision that I did not take lightly. At first, I hesitated to add images of my younger self, but as the book evolved, the first-person "I" became more prominent in the narrative, and I believed that readers might appreciate a sense of who I was (or at least what I looked like). If I could do it over, I would limit myself to one or two key images, only because it felt a bit self-indulgent to include more than this and it drew the reader's attention to the ethnographer and not to the ethnography. Even if your narrative justifies it, keep personal photos to a minimum. Your author's photo should suffice, unless you are writing a memoir. For example, in her recent book, *Traveling Heavy*, Ruth Behar complements the text with images of her childhood, and they elegantly capture the lost Cuba of her youth.

For my most recent manuscript, *The Left Side of History*, I found myself in the unfamiliar territory of the historical narrative and the confusing world of archival imagery. I obtained permission to reprint photos from the personal collections of my elderly informants or from their close living relatives. My primary informant, Elena Lagadinova, had an extensive collection of photos from all periods of her life and shared them with no reservations. The photos from her collection make up the bulk of the historical photos in the book and provide a wonderful sense of World War II and its aftermath in Bulgaria.

But other images proved difficult to include. In one chapter, I wanted to add an image of the young Iris Murdoch, Frank Thompson's Oxford love interest, and the woman who convinced him to join the Communist Party of Great Britain in 1938. I searched Wikimedia Commons and various free stock photography sites to find a public domain image of Iris Murdoch. In the end, only Getty Images had the perfect photo of the young Murdoch in 1939, so I contacted them to figure out how much it would cost to reprint it in an academic book. Duke University Press had some sort of deal with them.

As I explored the Getty Images website, I marveled at the various packages that I could buy. Prices depended on how many copies of my book would be printed, whether the image would be used on

Elena with the Bulgarian Partisans in 1944. Photo used with permission of Elena Lagadinova.

the inside or outside of the book, and a variety of other factors that seemed irrelevant to an academic title. I finally managed to get in touch with a representative who said I had to register for an account online if I wanted to receive a price for that one image. I did this and asked to use the image for an unlimited duration of time on the inside of an English language book that could be distributed internationally, but would not exceed a lifetime print run of 5,000, including e-books. The representative informed me that these rights for that one photo would cost $364, money that would come out of my own pocket. If Iris Murdoch had been a central figure in my book, I would have paid the fee, but I decided against it. Most academic books do not sell enough copies to justify such an expense.

There was another historical image, however, that I felt compelled to include. Readers needed to understand that Frank Thompson and the Bulgarian partisans fighting against their own government during World War II also fought against Nazi Germany. I could not

Adolf Hitler greets King Boris III of Bulgaria in Berlin after the Bulgarians join the Axis forces.
Photo courtesy of the United States Memorial Holocaust Museum.

expect a lay reader to know that Bulgaria was an Axis country, and this alliance underpinned the larger argument of the book. I looked everywhere for images of Hitler with Bulgaria's king, Tsar Boris III, but Getty and Corbis charge plump sums for images of Der Führer. In the end, I found the perfect photo on the website of the US Holocaust Memorial Museum, an image showing Adolf Hitler greeting Boris III in Berlin, a visual representation of a crucial component of my argument.

The image was in the public domain, and all I had to do was pay the US Holocaust Museum a $20 fee to send me a high-resolution copy by e-mail. They only asked that I acknowledge them as the source of the photo. Many images now reside in the public domain, but the responsibility lies with the author to prove this to the press. If you screw up, most university press contracts stipulate that the author is liable for any copyright infringement. In the case of the

Boris III and Hitler image, the US Holocaust Memorial Museum website stated that the image was in the public domain, so I only had to forward the relevant URL to the press. In recent years, the British Library has released millions of images to the public domain, setting an example for other museums and libraries, and making it easier for future ethnographers to find suitable images for their work.

Always include maps if you can, especially when you write about a little known country or region. You can hire a professional cartographer to draw a map for you, but today websites like D-Maps.com make it easy to download map templates to edit on your own. There may be other visuals such as charts or diagrams to help your reader navigate the information presented in your book. In most cases, you can design these at home and send them to the press for final manipulation. I enlist students and younger members of my family to help me navigate new graphic design programs.

If you know that you want to include maps, diagrams, or images in your text, make sure you ask for them when you negotiate your book contract or the word length of your journal article. In his book *Getting It Published*, William Germano suggests mentioning the number of images in your initial proposal. Images take up space, and the higher the number of images, the shorter your final text may have to be. This is a worthwhile trade-off. Also, most ethnographic books or journals cannot afford to print color images. Very rarely, an author might be able to negotiate for a small color gallery, but there has to be a clear and compelling reason to do so. In most cases, you must ensure that the meaning of your print images comes across in black and white, and hope you can include some color images on the book's website.

CHAPTER 8

Minimize Scientism

Many social scientists have natural science envy and try to make their writing appear more "scientific." In general, social scientists study human behavior whereas natural scientists study phenomena independent of the whims and desires of individuals. Different disciplinary conventions govern the language and style of writing in all fields of knowledge production, but there are some conventions that originated in the natural sciences and migrated to the social sciences. Two of these are the prolific use of technical terminologies and author-date citation.

Excise Jargon

Natural scientists deploy a robust vocabulary of specialized words for their observations of the natural world, and this makes many scientific articles difficult to read for those outside of the discipline. The language of quantum mechanics is difficult to grasp because quantum mechanics is difficult to grasp. The complexity of the language often mirrors the complexity and specialized nature of the field of study. Unfortunately, too many scholars believe that otherwise accessible fields of study, such as anthropology, sociology, or political science, require technical terminologies to describe concepts that could be rendered in plain English.

A great example comes from *The Sociological Imagination*, where

C. Wright Mills dedicates his entire second chapter to exposing the pretenses of "grand theory" in his discipline. Mills dissects Talcott Parsons's seminal book, *The Social System*, translating the great sociologist's convoluted prose into ordinary English. Mills begins his subversion with a few incisive questions:

> Is grand theory merely a confused verbiage or is there, after all, also something there? The answer, I think, is: Something is there, buried deep to be sure, but still something is being said. So the question becomes: After all the impediments to meaning are removed from grand theory and what is intelligible becomes available, what, then, is being said?[1]

Mills takes several jargon-laden paragraphs of Parsons's writing and reduces them to a few simple, declarative sentences. After presenting his interpretation, Mills declares, "In translating the contents of *The Social System* into English, I do not pretend that my translation is excellent, but only that in the translation no explicit meaning is lost. This—I am asserting—contains all that is intelligible in it."[2]

In my first class in graduate school, the professor made us read an excerpt from the second chapter of *The Sociological Imagination*. I remember my incredulity as I read Mills's translation of Parsons's paragraphs. Why would anyone intentionally write in such a deliberately opaque style? The graduate school newbies were perplexed. Professor Noguera predicted then that many of us would be writing like Parsons by the end of the year. None believed him, but I knew he was right six months later when I found myself writing about "the discursive construction of educative intersubjectivities."

Too many graduate students and junior professors reproduce disciplinary jargon because they think it makes them sound smart. Howard Becker, in his helpful book *Writing for Social Scientists*, has inveighed against convoluted prose for years, but with little success. Many social scientists believe that big words mean big brains. Ethnographers prove no exception. Recent books and articles are cluttered with clever neologisms and smattered with the intellectually fashionable terms of the moment. Like lawyers ensuring their own necessity through the production of *legalese*, scholars perpetuate their careers by hiding the paucity of their original ideas in fogs of *academese*. Jargon serves a purpose at times, and professional vocabularies provide an important means of scholarly communication. Complex concepts require special terms, and ethnographers need to maintain an analytical distinction between folk categories and the theoretical abstractions that help explain these categories. Furthermore, terms have histories that identify intellectual traditions: use "biopolitics" and you channel Foucault; use "habitus" and you channel Bourdieu; use "performativity" and you channel Butler. The problem arises when scholars decide to create new terms for ordinary concepts, or when they repurpose words or dismantle them to reveal the meaninglessness of language.

This tendency blossomed first among postmodernists. Anyone who attended grad school in the 1990s will remember the "I/eye," the random use of parentheses—(dis)ease, (dis)location, or dis(color)-ation—and the ubiquity of scare quotes around nouns, because a "tree" wasn't really a tree but just a word for "tree." Ethnographers enjoyed "problematizing" and "historicizing" every discourse or narrative they encountered. Postmodern language became the target of much academic humor and a major academic scandal when the postmodern cultural studies journal *Social Text* published a nonsense article by physicist Alan Sokal in 1996.[3] There still exists a postmodern generator,[4] which produces a random postmodernist article each time it loads. These have titles like: "Neodialectic Theories: Submaterialist textual theory and subdeconstructive textual theory," and "The Dialectic of Consensus: Poststructural dialectic theory, nihilism and Foucaultist power relations." The University of Chicago writing program maintains a random generator that lets you "write your own academic sentence."[5] From four drop down menus you choose words or phrases to populate the sentence. This website produces real gems like: "The epistemology of praxis furnishes a provisional lens for the analysis of the historicization of linguistic transparency" and "The logic of post-capitalist hegemony recapitulates the authentication of the specular economy."

To be fair, some scholars argue that complicated language jolts us out of lazy thinking. Ethnographers need to distance themselves from the everyday assumptions contained in the meanings of ordinary words. Seeing the world in different ways requires effort, and particular forms of writing force our brains to strain against the complacency of the things we think we already know. Some sophisticated social theorists use complex and circuitous sentences to illustrate their theoretical arguments about how language structures understanding. Unorthodox syntax can destabilize preconceived notions and produce opportunities for more profound analytic insight, but too often authors deploy jargon-filled writing to promote trivial insights to the status of high theory.

For decades, academics have suspected their peers of pulling wool over eyes. In his book, *Style: Ten Lessons in Clarity and Grace* (first published in 1981), Joseph Williams tells us that:

> Some writers choose complicated language not only to plump up their ideas, but to mask their absence, hoping that complexity will impress those who confuse difficulty with substance. When we don't know what we're talking about and don't want anyone else to know that we don't, we typically throw up a screen of big words in long, complicated sentences.[6]

In his brilliant 1961 essay on how to *fake* your way to success in academia ("The Academic Con-Men: Advice to Young College Professors"), Francis J. Kerins asserts:

> One cardinal rule is to be obscure—consciously, conscientiously, and constantly obscure. The number of people who can distinguish between obscurity and profundity is startlingly, and for your purposes fortunately, small. You should develop a jargon of your own; either make up words yourself or use ordinary words in entirely new and unclear meanings.[7]

Although Kerins was writing a satirical piece, the humor of his article rests in its prescience. Even back in the early 1960s, when universities were flush with cash after the Soviet launch of Sputnik, Kerins could poke fun at the academic frauds that populated the ivory tower, hiding behind their deliberately obtuse prose.

And this was not a phenomenon limited to the United States. In the back of his 2006 book, *Breaking the Spell,* Daniel Dennett recounts the following conversation between the philosophers John Searle and Michel Foucault (the big daddy of postmodernism):

> John Searle once told me about a conversation he had with the late Michel Foucault: "Michel, you're so clear in conversation; why is your written work so obscure?" To which Foucault replied, "That's because, in order to be taken seriously by French philosophers, twenty-five percent of what you write has to be impenetrable nonsense." I have coined a term for this tactic, in honour of Foucault's candor: *eumerdification.*[8]

Dennett's term "*eumerdification*" roughly translates as "*shittifying,*" or the act of inserting approximately 25 percent crap into academic writing to make it sound academic. With so many esteemed writers and scholars poking fun at this tendency, why does obscure language persist? Because it works.

The proclivity to obfuscate permeates almost all of the social sciences whose practitioners fear that the hard won results of their research are either trivial or false. I once sat on an interdisciplinary fellowship panel that reviewed an erudite proposal from a graduate student in anthropology. Since several of the panelists read the proposal twice and still had difficulty understanding the project, they assumed theoretical sophistication. Channeling C. Wright Mills, a third panel member translated the proposal into plain English. Once stripped of its verbosity, the proposal revealed inherent weaknesses, and the selection panel ranked it accordingly. Had that panel member not been present, the proposal might have been funded over worthier ones. I learned that day that fancy language intimidates readers outside of a discipline. No one wants to be the one person who doesn't understand a particular proposal or article, and few scholars will risk saying that the emperor has no clothes.

Thus, there are only four reasons to write your ethnography in highly theoretical, obscurantist language:

1. You are writing your dissertation and your advisor and other committee members expect this.
2. You are targeting your book or article for a narrow and defined subset of your scholarly peers who know and understand your jargon.
3. You have discovered a deep social truth and are genuinely trying to destabilize your readers' understandings of the meanings implicit in ordinary language.
4. You are writing to impress upon strangers outside of your immediate disciplinary subfield that you have a command of technical terminology and can produce profound and original insights through the strategic manipulation of language.

Confidence and bluster can get you far in academia. Junior scholars are motivated more by self-preservation than by deceit when they reproduce intentionally difficult language to throw smokescreens over their ho-hum ideas. It's a tough business and we should be sympathetic. If, however, you are secure in the originality of your findings and certain that the evidence you have collected substantiates them, you have no reason to hide your results or bury your insights among neologisms. Aim for clarity and concision, even if this sounds less "scientific."

Consider Endnotes

Most students and scholars learn disciplinary conventions regarding citation and never think about them again. But citation practices vary widely both between and within disciplines, and once you survive the dissertation you enjoy more flexibility in choosing your citation style. To be sure, academic journals have their own house styles for articles. The 2009 style guide for all journals of the American Anthropological Association states: "All references must be cited in author-date form; all author-date citations must be referenced."[9] The guide provides instructions for how to reference different media. Similarly, the American Sociological Association sells a style manual to teach aspiring sociologists to use the author-date citation format in combination with a reference list. The ASA guide elucidates how to use the author-date format for e-mails, websites, brochures, and other eclectic materials. Political science, economics, cultural geography, and psychology also demand the in-text, author-date citation style.

Where did these conventions come from? The standard of in-text author-date citation derives from something called the "Harvard style," which originated in the field of zoology. In 1881 the zoologist Edward Laurens Mark published an important paper on the garden slug wherein he included the first parenthetical author-date citation (Mark 1881). This system spread out from zoology to other natural sciences where the author's name and the date of the publication comprise the two most important pieces of information. Prior to Mark's invention of the author-date referencing system, footnotes were sprinkled randomly throughout the text and marked off by asterisks and other printer's marks. The author-date system streamlined citations, favoring brevity and clarity. As those working in the social and behavioral fields increasingly aspired to be considered "scientists," they adopted the author-date system. Footnotes and endnotes seemed too humanistic for hard-boiled anthropologists, sociologists, political scientists, economists, and psychologists. Parenthetical citations proliferated throughout social scientific publications, ensuring that the work appeared more like biology than like history or literature.

Although journal style guidelines and dissertation norms dictate author-date citations, ethnographers should consider using endnotes whenever possible. Alfred Kroeber once said that "anthropology is the most humanistic of the sciences and the most scientific of the humanities," and the kind of qualitative research methods that inform the writing of ethnography places the genre even further on the humanities side of the humanities–natural sciences spectrum. Endnotes distract less than author-date citations, which have the effect of constantly reminding that the article or book is a scholarly treatise not meant for popular consumption. An in-text citation breaks the reader's concentration in two ways: by visually interrupting the flow of the text and by making her wonder "who is this Carlisle person referred to in the citation?" when she's trying to think about the meaning of the text and probably doesn't even care who Carlisle is.

Author-date citations are also ill suited to the citation of works that have multiple editions (e.g., Marx [1848] 1974), or to prolific authors who publish multiple articles or books in the same year (e.g., Slavoj Žižek 2009a, 2009b, 2009c, 2009d). Author-date citations also prove unwieldy when citing nonacademic references such as legal documents, websites, newspaper articles, blog posts, tweets, brochures, pamphlets, or other sources where it is either difficult or impossible to identify an author or a date. The most frustrating example of this is when I am trying to cite articles from *The Economist* magazine where none of the individual articles have bylines. If you must use the author-date style, ensure that you place them at the end of the sentence or paragraph rather than right in the middle.

Although I follow journal style guides for articles, I always use endnotes in my books. I wrote my dissertation with the requisite author-date citations, and it was in dialogue with my first editor at Duke University Press that I switched to endnotes as I revised the thesis into a book. Making the change from author-date to endnotes was a tedious process in those days before citation management software, but today I could press a button. Endnotes welcome nonspecialist and undergraduate readers who know little about the scholarly debates in your field.

As I wrote this chapter, I pulled down a few armloads of books from my shelves to investigate the relative distribution of author-date versus endnote citations. David Valentine's *Imagining Transgender*, Katherine Verdery's *The Vanishing Hectare*, Amy Borovoy's *The Too-Good Wife*, Carla Freeman's *High Tech and High Heels*, and Tom

Boellstorff's *Coming of Age in Second Life* all used in text author-date citations. On the other hand, Ruth Behar's *Translated Woman* uses endnotes, as do Paul Stoller's *Embodying Colonial Memories: Spirit Possession, Power, and the Hauka in West Africa* and Michael Herzfeld's *Evicted From Eternity: The Restructuring of Modern Rome* and *The Body Impolitic: Artisans and Artifice in the Global Hierarchy of Value.* In *Body and Soul,* sociologist Loïc Wacquant uses footnotes, as do Anne Allison and Esther Newton in *Nightwork* and *Mother Camp,* respectively. A variety of different presses published these books, and even books published by the same press contained different citation formats.

My brief survey shows that, at least for books, authors choose their citation format. If you are in a position to make a choice, do not blindly follow disciplinary conventions because you think it will make your work appear more scientific. Citations exist so you can acknowledge the ideas that influenced your work and recognize the scholars who preceded you. They also elaborate on ideas in the text and point the reader to relevant further reading. Citation format matters less than including the necessary information.

CHAPTER 9

Unclutter Your Prose

"Omit needless words," admonish William Strunk, Jr. and E. B. White in their classic book, *The Elements of Style*. Never has there been a more succinct and valuable piece of advice, particularly for academics prone to wordiness. And we're no longer talking about disciplinary jargon, but rather the sheer proliferation of surplus words. Strunk and White advise:

> Vigorous writing is concise. A sentence should contain no unnecessary words, a paragraph no unnecessary sentences, for the same reason that a drawing should have no unnecessary lines and a machine no unnecessary parts. This requires not that the writer make all his sentences short, or that he avoid all detail and treat his subjects only in outline, but that every word tell.[1]

Similarly, George Orwell provides a list of handy rules for writers in his well-known 1946 essay, "Politics and the English Language." Like Strunk and White, Orwell believed that our written language required liberation from excess verbiage. Orwell's rules include:

> Never use a long word where a short one will do.
> If it is possible to cut a word out, always cut it out.
> Never use the passive where you can use the active.
> Never use a foreign phrase, a scientific word, or a jargon word if you can think of an everyday English equivalent.[2]

William Zinsser, too, believes our language has been weighed down by sheer wordiness: "Clutter is the disease of American writing. We are a society strangling in unnecessary words, circular constructions, pompous frills and meaningless jargon."[3]

Unfortunately, many scholars believe that big words are better than small ones, that longer sentences are better than short ones, and that bulging paragraphs are better than trim ones. Compare the following two sentences:

1. Due to the fact that most Romanians believe that their political leaders are generally corrupt, Romanians as a whole tend to distrust their politicians.
2. Romanians distrust their politicians, believing they are corrupt.

These sentences communicate the same idea, but the second does so in eight words where the first takes twenty-four. In most cases, the inexperienced scholar writes the first sentence because he has not gone back to edit his work.

But there are other cases, of increasing frequency in the social sciences, where authors insert filler sentences to round out the word count of an LPU, or "least publishable unit."[4] The LPU, also known as the SPU (smallest publishable unit) or the MPU (minimum publishable unit) is the least amount of information a scholar can put into an article and still have it accepted by a peer-reviewed journal in his field (yet another invention of the natural sciences that drifted into the social sciences). Scholars break up their research into the smallest publishable units possible to increase the total number of publications listed on their CVs. A friend of mine in political science confides that she never includes more than one original idea in an article; if she finds herself writing a piece with two major contributions to the literature, she divides her research and writes two shorter pieces instead of one long one. The LPU proliferates in sociology, economics, and psychology. While I understand the rationalization for LPUs, they promote bad writing. Extra words become bubble wrap for one precious idea being prepared for publication.

Ethnographers face the opposite problem. Even when writing LPUs, we run up against hard upper word limits. Substantiating arguments with ethnographic data takes space, and you can cut a long essay by tightening your prose. Imagine if you could shorten one sentence in each paragraph from twenty-four words to eight without losing any meaning. But you must ensure that no meaning is lost. Strunk and White tell us to "omit needless words" not just to "omit words." In ethnography words can be quite "needful." There will be plenty of cases where the deletion of one word (an adverb or adjective) requires the insertion of whole sentences to replace it. If this brings depth and detail to your text, then it is a good trade off even if it ups your word count. To captivate the reader you must pack your information into clean and succinct prose that enlightens but does not overwhelm. In the remainder of this chapter, I will focus on a few tips and tricks to help you identify the *needless* words in your writing.

Use One-Dollar Words Instead of Ten-Dollar Words

William Faulkner once criticized Ernest Hemingway's simple and straightforward style by saying that Hemingway never used words "that might send a reader to a dictionary." In response, Hemingway said, "Poor Faulkner. Does he really think big emotions come from big words? He thinks I don't know the ten-dollar words. I know them all right. But there are older and simpler and better words, and those are the ones I use."[5]

"Verbose," "prolix," "logorrheic," "grandiloquent," and "garrulous" are all wonderful synonyms for "wordy," but why not just say "wordy" if you mean wordy? Most scholars believe that "grandiloquent" evokes more intelligence than "wordy." But a 2006 study by Daniel Oppenheimer showed that when Stanford students read needlessly complex writing, their rating of the author's intelligence decreased.[6] Students reviewed a wide variety of written texts including personal statements, dissertation abstracts in sociology, and philosophical essays. Oppenheimer found that clarity and succinctness positively correlated with ratings of author intelligence. Across a wide variety of circumstances, students perceived more smarts from authors who used simpler words.

The caveat is that D. M. Oppenheimer tested students (not scholarly peers), and he tested the effect of *unnecessarily* complex words. He writes:

> [T]here are many times when a long word is appropriate, because it is more precise or concise. These studies primarily investigated the use of needless complexity in writing. When a long word is actually the best word for the occasion, it may be that using it will lead to positive appraisals. Indeed, these studies cannot rule out the possibility that in some situations judicious use of a thesaurus will improve the quality of writing.[7]

So you must be able to tell the difference between the needless and "needful" ten-dollar words in your own prose. Go through your work and circle all of the ten-dollar words you find. If you can think of a simpler substitute for a complex word, then make the substitution as long as no meaning or nuance gets lost. If you are using a ten-dollar word because it accurately describes, leave it in. If you find yourself using lots of ten-dollar words, revisit your paragraphs and see if you can rephrase things to include a smattering of good one-dollar words. Clarity demands one-dollar words, but concision requires some ten-dollar specimens. Find a balance.

Avoid Common Filler Phrases

Academics love to use phrases such as "due to the fact that" or "in order to," and I serially offend in this regard. I cannot help writing these filler phrases; my brain just produces them. In my first drafts I allow them to flow, but I always go back and strike them out. Notice the difference between these sentences:

1. Due to the fact that she was lonely, Miranda went home with Jim.
2. Since Miranda was lonely, she went home with Jim.

1. With the hope of increasing her popularity, Caroline pretended to enjoy pop music.
2. To increase her popularity, Caroline pretended to enjoy pop music.

In *Style*, Joseph Williams includes a list of common phrases that can be replaced with one word. For instance, "the reason for," "for the reason that," "in light of these facts," and "considering these facts" can all be replaced with the words "because" or "since." "Despite the fact that" or (my favorite) "In spite of the fact that" can both be replaced with a simple "although." The word "if" can substitute for the phrases "under circumstances in which" or "in a situation in which." "It is important that," "it is essential that," or "it is crucial that" are phrases that stand in for "must" or "should." Replace "the ways in which" with the word "how." Again, examine these two sentences:

1. It is essential that the reader take note of the important difference between bribes and political gifting.
2. The reader should note the important difference between bribes and political gifting.

In the editing process, search for these filler phrases and cut them out. They add no clarity, and much clutter, to your prose.

Avoid the Passive Voice

Compare the sentences in these pairs:

1. The paper was graded by the graduate student.
2. The graduate student graded the paper.

1. The book prize was won by a Venezuelan anthropologist.
2. A Venezuelan anthropologist won the book prize.

The great writing experts all inveigh against the passive voice (if Microsoft Word's squiggly green lines weren't enough). Aside from certain appropriate circumstances, the passive bores the reader. Use of the passive voice also adds extra words, which can be cut by rewriting the sentence in an active formation. More importantly, the passive voice can serve as a vehicle for unsubstantiated generalizations. For instance, I can write that:

1. The Bulgarian peasants were historically marginalized.
2. The Roma in Europe are discriminated against.

Although grammatically correct, the sentences require further explanation or they remain mere assertions. In both cases, no actor gets identified. We do not know who has been marginalizing the peasants or discriminating against the Roma. In George Orwell's 1946 essay, he recognized that politicians employed the passive voice to avoid taking responsibility for their actions. A classic example used and abused by Washington politicians for decades is the sentence "mistakes were made," deployed most famously by Ronald Reagan in 1987 during the Iran-Contra affair. It proves easier to say "mistakes were made," than to utter the words, "I made a mistake." Orwell saw the regeneration of the English language as the first step in the political regeneration of true democracy.

In academia, the passive voice can cover for sloppy research or for an unwillingness to name a particular set of actors (perhaps because this might be perceived as politically incorrect). Here are the two sentences above rendered in the active voice:

1. The Ottoman sultans and the Greek Orthodox clergy historically marginalized the Bulgarian peasants.
2. Both Eastern and Western Europeans discriminate against the Roma.

In the first version of sentence one, the reader does not know who marginalized the Bulgarian peasantry. For all we know it is the Bulgarian bourgeoisie. The active voice forces the author to tell the reader who the oppressors are, and in this case it is not other Bulgarians, a fact that Greek or Turkish historians might want to occlude. Similarly in the second version of the second sentence, naming of the actors refocuses the readers' attention away from the victims of discrimination and onto the perpetrators of that discrimination, a political act in itself.

Feminists have long argued against the way newspapers report rape cases: "Fifteen-year-old girl was raped on school playground," or "Waitress raped in a parking lot." The use of the passive tense focuses all of the attention on the victim of the crime and not on the person who committed it. The active construction (even when details of the suspect are unknown)—"Unidentified male rapes teenager on school playground" or "Police searching for man who raped waitress in parking lot"—shifts the reader's focus from the acted upon to the actor, a subtle rhetorical difference that affects how readers understand the news and how they might be motivated to react to it.

In the university setting, one hears the phrases: "The assistant professor was denied tenure" or "The faculty handbook was changed to lengthen the academic year." These passive constructions also occlude the actors: "Her colleagues in the English department voted against the assistant professor for tenure" or "The administration has modified the faculty handbook to lengthen the academic year." Avoiding the passive voice might create a circumstance where adding in an actor requires more words. But if extra words clarify your meaning, they are no indulgence.

Despite all the foregoing, there may be good reason to use the passive voice in a particular sentence. If you want to focus on the object of a verb, deploy the passive. When I write that "Barack Obama was elected President" I am emphasizing *who* was elected rather than who did the electing, in this case, the American people. "Meryl Streep was awarded an Oscar" places the focus on the actress rather than the nameless members of the Academy who did the awarding. Of course, you could write, "Barack Obama *won* the presidential election" or "Meryl Street *won* an Oscar," which are both active sentences. But you might want to vary the style and rhythm of your sentences. Sometimes the passive voice allows you to place the more important information at the end of a sentence to create a more fluid narrative. I will discuss these syntagmatic issues in the next chapter. For now, watch for the passive voice when its elimination helps you omit needless words.

Avoid Excess Repetition of Your Argument

Beginning ethnographers often repeat their main argument several times throughout an article, dissertation, or book. In articles it is common to lay out your main thesis in the introduction and to restate it in your conclusion, but some ethnographers like to remind their readers of their primary insight after each anecdote or fieldnote excerpt substantiating their main point. Overkill. Allow your evidence to build over the course of your article and then gather it together and pack a rhetorical punch at the end. For a book-length project, you may be tempted to plant signposts for the reader at the beginning and end of each chapter: "In this chapter I will show . . ." or "In this chapter I have shown. . . ." Although some subtle signposting proves useful, this dissertation habit can be overdone. Don't patronize the reader's intelligence.

Once again, find the middle ground. You want to make sure the reader follows your argument without making them feel like you distrust their ability to see the connections between arguments and evidence. Watch for places where you repeat the same thing using different words. Keep a running tally of how often you state your argument, and consider this number in relation to the ultimate length of your manuscript. If you are restating your thesis more than once every twenty pages, you probably need to do less telling and more showing in your writing.

CHAPTER 10

Master Good Grammar and Syntax

In the fall of 2011, I joined my first, nonacademic writing group. Our membership numbered four: a poet, a journalist, a novelist, and me. We toiled away on individual projects and met once a month to share updates on our work and read each other a few pages. As a favor, I asked Sarah Braunstein, the novelist, to read a draft of my manuscript for *The Left Side of History*. Although she enjoyed learning about the history of World War II in the Balkans, Sarah told me that I had "weak verbs."

"I have what?" I said.

"Weak verbs."

My heart sank. I had already published three books. How was I just learning this now?

"Why are my verbs weak?" I said. "I didn't know verbs could be weak."

Sarah proceeded to enlighten me on the various tips and tricks that teachers in creative writing programs use to invigorate prose.

Buy one of the classic style guides for writers. I have included a list of these in the suggested reading section at the back of this book, but my favorites include Strunk and White's *The Elements of Style*, William Zinsser's *On Writing Well*, and Joseph Williams' *Style: Toward Clarity and Grace*. Since neither of my parents spoke English as their first language (my mom spoke Spanish, my dad Farci), I did not learn grammar rules intuitively. Although I was born and raised in the

United States, and we all spoke English to each other at home, I realized at some point that *bad* English was our common language,
and that my budding vocabulary was peppered with Spanglish and
crypto-Farci-isms. I took matters into my own hands and devoured
stylebooks like a hungry basset hound gobbles unguarded meatballs.
To write readable ethnographies, master the grammar of the English
language. Develop a working knowledge of what makes for good sentence structure. This short chapter cannot explore all of the ground
covered in good style guides, but I provide the most important bits
of advice I have gleaned over the years, starting, of course, with the
difference between weak and strong verbs.

Use Strong Verbs

A weak verb includes any version of "to be" or "to have"—is, are,
was, were, will be, has, had, have had, and will have. Much academic
prose staggers under the weight of weak verbs. Before Sarah's remark,
I never noticed the proliferation of weak verbs in my writing. I possessed no idea that verbs could be weak or strong, and I failed to com-
prehend why better verbs made for better writing. Sarah told me that
in her classes, she advises her students to take a piece of their writing
and circle all of the verbs on the first page. Most students marvel at
the number of weak verbs that populate their texts.

After concerted effort, I produced the previous four sentences
with strong verbs. Now I am going to show you those same sentences
as I originally wrote them (with weak verbs):

> Much academic prose *is* weighed down with the weight of weak verbs.
> Before Sarah's remark, I *had* never noticed how many weak verbs
> there *were* in my writing. Indeed, I *had* no idea that verbs could *be*
> weak or strong, and it *was* hard for me to understand why better verbs
> made for better writing. Sarah told me that in her writing classes, she
> advises her students to take a piece of their writing and circle all of the
> verbs on the first page. Most students *are* amazed at the number of
> weak verbs that populate their texts.

Taking Sarah's advice I circled all of my weak verbs. I replaced "is weighed down" with "staggers under the weight of." "I *had* never noticed how many weak verbs there *were* in my writing" became "I never noticed the proliferation of weak verbs in my writing." In the last sentence, "most students are amazed at" became "most students marvel at."

Using stronger verbs allows you to omit more words and bring vigor and variety to your prose. If you Google "strong verbs," the Internet serves up detailed lists of words that you can use instead of common verbs like "to be," "to have," "to take," or "to go." These days I keep a running list of good verbs on my computer. I dip into the list whenever I find myself stuck on some version of "to be." When reading, I notice that most journalists and fiction writers do their best to deploy strong verbs whereas academics fall back on the weak ones. As an exercise, read a newspaper article. Circle all of the verbs. Then pick up a piece of academic writing and do the same. The difference becomes clear.

Using the passive voice also promotes the proliferation of weak verbs. Consider these sentence pairs:

1. The figure *is* derived by scientists re-examining old data.
2. Scientists *calculate* the figure by re-examining old data.

1. Students *are* graded on their in-class participation.
2. The professor *evaluates* students on their in-class participation.

1. The academic coordinator *was* confused by the new registration procedures.
2. The new registration procedures *baffled* the academic coordinator.

In all three examples above, the more interesting verbs "calculate," "evaluate," and "baffle" replace passive formations using "is," "are," and "was." The exercise of circling your verbs exposes instances of the passive voice that you may have not noticed before.

Academic writers also overuse the present continuous and the past continuous tenses. I fall into this trap all of the time (e.g., I *am falling* in this trap all of the time). When I read my daily free-writing pages where I dump thoughts on paper without a care for spelling, grammar, or syntax, I cringe at the proliferation of the *-ing* words. Overuse of the past perfect tense (*I had worked, I had traveled*, or *I had prepared*) presents another common pitfall. Much better to write: "I worked," "I traveled," and "I prepared." Of course, occasions occur when you need to use the past continuous or the past perfect to capture a sequence of events, or to vary syntax in a paragraph. Too much simple past or present tense becomes boring, so good writers know when to slip in the passive voice or an alternative tense for variety. Just don't overuse any one form.

Examine this paragraph from one of my recent grant proposals:

> The project that I *am proposing* examines the inner workings of one state socialist women's organization and its ongoing attempts to train and mobilize women from the developing world.... In the last four years, I *have been doing* research in the archives of the Women's International Democratic Federation, which coordinated the efforts of all state socialist women's organizations and worked closely with Bulgarian women between 1945 and 1990. I *have also been working* in the archives of the Committee of the Movement of Bulgarian Women.

Not only do I overuse words ending in *-ing*, I also tend to favor the present perfect tense, which adds needless words. Taking Sarah's advice, I now circle *-ing* verbs when I edit my work. I can tighten a paragraph by reformulating my sentences around the simple past or present tense. I rewrote the paragraph like this:

> *My project* examines the inner workings of one state socialist women's organization and its ongoing attempts to train and mobilize women from the developing world.... For the last four years, I *conducted research* in the archives of the Women's International Democratic Federation, which coordinated the efforts of all state socialist women's

organizations and collaborated with Bulgarian women between 1945 and 1990. I *also worked* in the archives of the Committee of the Movement of Bulgarian Women.

Notice how "the project that I am proposing examines" becomes "my project examines," and how "I have been doing research" changed to "I conducted research." I omitted needless words and replaced weak verbs with strong ones. I also axed the use of the present continuous and past continuous tenses. These seem small changes, but they make a big difference in the finished product. Learning to identify writing quirks improves your prose. Weak verbs and weak conjugations of those verbs make for weak writing. Spend time thinking about your word choices, and liven up your pages.

Keep Subjects and Verbs Close Together

Keep the subject of a sentence as close to its verb as possible. This may sound intuitive, but you have no idea how often academic writers violate the rule. Consider this sentence:

> The results of a study proving that using needlessly big words in academic writing makes you sound less intelligent will be published today.

In this sentence, fourteen words separate the subject—"study"—from the weak verb in the passive construction: "will be published." Ethnographic writing chokes on convoluted sentences, and yet they proliferate like requests for letters of recommendation in September. I can rewrite this unwieldy specimen in a more user-friendly style by placing the subject and verb at the beginning of the sentence and banishing the passive voice:

> Today, researchers will publish the results of a study proving that using needlessly big words in academic writing makes you sound less intelligent.

Whenever you find yourself rereading a sentence, go back and examine the space between the subject and the verb. Often, the author inserts explanatory detail between the subject and the verb, believing that readers need to know the "why" of an action before they know what that action is.

Compare these two sentences:

1. The ethnographer who was homesick and decided that she was not learning anything new from her fieldwork returned to London two months earlier than planned.
2. The ethnographer returned to London two months earlier than planned because she felt homesick and believed her fieldwork had nothing new to teach her.

In the first sentence, a fifteen-word dependent clause explaining the subject's motivation separates the subject "ethnographer" from the verb "returned." This formulation confuses the reader because he doesn't yet know what verb the dependent clause modifies. The second sentence puts the subject and the verb at the beginning of the sentence and uses the subordinating conjunction "because" to introduce the explanation for the action. In this way, readers first get the *what* and then the *why*, a sentence structure that flows naturally from the way we speak in conversation. But perhaps you want to emphasize the *why*, to foreground the explanation for a subsequent action. You can still accomplish this by keeping the subject and verb together:

Homesick and believing that she was not learning anything new from her fieldwork, the ethnographer returned to London two months earlier than planned.

If you want to vary your syntax, playing with the placement of dependent clauses provides a nice trick for switching things up. Just ensure that your subjects and verbs stay cozy.

Vary Your Sentence Length

In his book, *On Writing Well*, William Zinsser explains that "there's not much to be said about the period except that most writers don't reach it soon enough." Ethnographers like long sentences. Lots of information can be packed into a sentence, especially when we are trying to interweave those juicy ethnographic details with complicated theoretical analysis. Longer sentences are necessarily complex compound sentences, and too many of them clutter writing. Shorter sentences tend to be simpler sentences, and some writers fear that simpler sentences can only communicate simple ideas. But complex ideas are best expressed in simpler constructions. Save straightforward information (such as descriptions of your methodology) for the complex sentences. Then learn to combine the two. Simple sentences make your writing clearer, but too many short sentences can become as dull as too many long sentences. In his book, *100 Ways to Improve Your Writing*, Gary Provost provides this wonderful example:

> This sentence has five words. Here are five more words. Five-word sentences are fine. But several together become monotonous. Listen to what is happening. The writing is getting boring. The sound of it drones. It's like a stuck record. The ear demands some variety. Now listen. I vary the sentence length, and I create music. Music. The writing sings. It has a pleasant rhythm, a lilt, a harmony. I use short sentences. And I use sentences of medium length. And sometimes, when I am certain the reader is rested, I will engage him with a sentence of considerable length, a sentence that burns with energy and builds with all the impetus of a crescendo, the roll of the drums, the crash of the cymbals–sounds that say listen to this, it is important.[1]

When you go back to revise, choose a few paragraphs at random and examine the length of your sentences. Count the words. Are they all uniform? If so, see if you can break some of the longer sentences up into two or three pieces. If you have a penchant for writing in a series of short, staccato sentences, use some conjunctions to string them together. Variety is the spice of life and of sentence writing.

Limit Adverbs and Adjectives

Fiction writers and journalists hate adverbs. Adjectives inspire little more respect. For the literati, the overuse of adverbs and adjectives separates the amateur writer from the professional. Horror writer Stephen King goes so far to claim that "the road to hell is paved with adverbs." As I have already discussed in the chapter on ethnographic detail, adverbs and adjectives can signal lazy writing. Replace "the professor walked swiftly to her office" with a verb that incorporates the meaning of the adverb, such as: "the professor hurried to her office" or "the professor dashed to her office."

Examine the following two lists:

touched gently	caressed
advised condescendingly	pontificated
considered quietly	pondered
breathed heavily	panted

In each of the cases, the verb on the right can replace the verb-adverb pair on the left. An even worse usage occurs when the adverbs repeat the meaning already contained in the verb, such as:

1. embraced lovingly
2. smiled happily
3. cried sadly

Most embraces result from love, most smiles result from happiness, and most tears result from melancholy. In each of these cases, the adverbs add nothing to the meaning of the verb. The best time (and some argue the only time) to use adverbs is when they modify the verb in a counterintuitive or unexpected way:

1. embraced stiffly
2. smiled miserably
3. cried joyously

If you have the space in your ethnographic writing, describe these actions of your informants in greater detail. For instance:

1. She put her arms around his shoulders, but made sure her chest did not touch his.
2. His faced twitched with anguish, but he contracted his cheek muscles into the semblance of a smile.
3. Tears streamed over her cheekbones as she threw her arms up toward the sky and sang out her thanks.

Alas, we often lack the space to describe every detail, and a well-chosen adverb can capture our intended meaning in a more succinct way. The advice to omit needless words sometimes conflicts with the injunction against adverbs, so each writer must decide for herself when and where to make use of these -ly words.

Experts deride adjectives less than adverbs, because adjectives modify nouns rather than verbs. Writing instructors still complain that adjectives provide shortcuts for writers unwilling or unable to specify the unique characteristic of their nouns. If I say that "the student wrote the perfect paper," I leave ambiguous my criteria for perfection. I could mean that the essay was faultless or exactly meeting my expectations, but the reader has no idea which one. A classic example of imprecise adjective usage is "my new car." This can refer to a car I bought new or a used car that is new to me.

For ethnographers, adjectives play an important role in thick description and we must choose them with care in our finished writing. When I go back and read my fieldnotes, I shrink at the proliferation of imprecise adjectives, but I know that these are only mnemonic devices to jog my memory later. When it comes time to write up my ethnographic data, I think long and hard about my adjectival choices. I circle adverbs and adjectives in key passages and do my best to render them as precise as possible. Good adjectives describe things that cannot be described through action: the celadon dress, the loose jowls, or the manicured lawn. Weak adjectives are too general or they describe character attributes that are better described through action.

The truth remains that adjectives are useful, as is the occasional adverb. They provide variety to my sentences and allow me to be succinct when I have other important matters to attend to. I understand the reasons for the bias against them, but I take umbrage at software programs that algorithmically flag every adverb for deletion. In the last sentence the adverb "algorithmically" qualifies as a good adverb in my book because it modifies the verb "flags," which is an action usually performed by humans. "Algorithmically" is also a precise adverb that leaves little ambiguity as to how the flagging is done—automatically and without consideration of each individual case. I know that writing instructors disagree, and that Stephen King thinks I am going to hell, but I accept that, *defiantly*.

Old Information before New Information (or the Passive Voice Revisited)

When constructing paragraphs, think of your sentences as chains linked to one another. One convention requires that you put old information at the beginning of your sentences and place new information at the end. By putting the old at the beginning, you remind the reader of things she already knows before you introduce another idea. Sometimes this strategy demands the use of the passive voice; clarity and coherence justify its use. Examine the following two examples:

1. Each day, the assistant professor enjoys three morning hours for research and writing. The department chair insists that the assistant professor take this time. The chair believes that assistant professors require protection from the demands of service and teaching.

2. Each week, the assistant professor enjoys three morning hours for research and writing. This research and writing time is granted at the insistence of the department chair. The chair believes that assistant professors require protection from the demands of service and teaching.

The second paragraph contains a middle sentence written in the passive tense, but it flows more naturally than the first paragraph. Even though the first paragraph contains three active sentences, the second paragraph employs the idea that new and old information should link sentences together. In the second paragraph the sentence "The department chair insists that the assistant professor have this time" becomes "This research and writing time is granted at the insistence of the department chair." The "research and writing time" links to the end of the first sentence and the "department chair" links to the beginning of the sentence that follows, creating smooth transitions. During the revision process, particularly in your analytical passages, consider how the strategic use of the passive voice might improve the flow of your ideas. Overuse of the passive voice spells doom for most ethnographic writing, but some paragraphs benefit from its selective deployment.

These five writing tips can go a long way to improve the quality of your ethnographic writing. Just remember to write first and revise later. Never let grammar or syntagmatic rules prevent you from bashing out that first draft.

CHAPTER 11

Revise!

I start this chapter with a confession. My first drafts suck. I choke on words. I litter my pages with adverbs and the passive voice, I tell instead of show, I write long, convoluted compound sentences with thirty-word dependent clauses separating my subjects from my verbs, and I never met a ten-dollar word that didn't infatuate me. I overuse weak verbs and the past continuous tense. I abuse semicolons. My first drafts contain such rubbish that after I edit them I wipe the blank space on my hard drive to make sure the originals can never be recovered.

Revision makes the writer, but editing lacks the glamour of writing. Editorial work fails to evoke an image of inspired artist or ingenious thinker. Like the goddess Athena emerging fully grown from the head of Zeus, beginners believe that good prose springs out, fully formed, from the minds of its authors. Nothing could be further from the truth. If you remember only one thing from this book, please let it be this: revise the hell out of everything you write. All of the advice contained in this book means nothing unless you take the time to work on your editing.

Revise your work in two stages. The first stage of revision tends to deal with overall structure and arguments—the big picture of your manuscript. This is what you do after you get feedback from friendly readers or after you have listened to your manuscript in its entirety. The second stage includes editing at the paragraph and sentence level, choosing better verbs and writing out the passive voice, sometimes called line editing. When revising your work, make sure you focus on the first stage before you get seduced by the line editing. Too many ethnographers waste time perfecting paragraphs and sentences that get cut from the text during a subsequent revision.

I love line editing despite the time commitment required. I feel the most creative when tinkering with a sentence or finding the perfect synonym. Editing brings the deep satisfaction that comes with practicing a craft, in this case the craft of writing. But many ethnographers feel overwhelmed by the task of editing an entire manuscript. In this chapter, I will outline some proven editing techniques that you can use to rework your writing. In the next chapter, I'll continue the discussion about revision when I explore writing rituals.

Write Your First Draft All the Way Through

Many doctoral students fail to earn their PhDs because they never finish their dissertations. They complete their coursework, pass their qualifying exams, and do all of their research, but writing the thesis proves an insurmountable barrier. Why does the dissertation present such a challenge? Because students can't push past the first chapter. Too many dissertators start with their introduction and find that they have nothing to say. Or they realize they have no idea what they are trying to introduce. Becoming a permanent ABD (all but dissertation) qualifies as a personal disaster for many aspiring ethnographers.

In Anne Lamott's brilliant book, *Bird by Bird: Some Instructions on Writing and Life*, the author advises all would-be writers to embrace what she calls the "shitty first draft." Decide what you're going to write, and then write it straight through without stopping. If you need to write an article, spend some time thinking of an abstract that captures the essence of your argument and the data you have to substantiate it. You can take a few days to put together a really good abstract. Once you have it, use it as your introductory paragraph and start writing. Keep putting words on the page until you reach what you think will be the end. Never go back and read what you have already written. This may seem difficult, but you can learn to let your thoughts flow. If you find yourself stuck at a section or in need of a particular fact or reference not at hand, leave placeholders in your text. Phrases like "insert quote here" or "discuss relevant studies here" litter my first drafts. If I need to stop working for the day, I always type the letters "XXX" in my electronic document. When I come back to the file, I open the document and search for the "XXX," thus bypassing the text I've previously written.

Writing straight through presents bigger challenges when working on a dissertation or book. My colleague, the anthropologist Doug Rogers, author of *The Old Faith and the Russian Land*, understands these challenges and still insists on writing as much as he can without revising. Doug writes:

> Given all of the revising and reclassifying that I practice and recommend, it's imperative for me to keep going, to put off the urge to rewrite and re-classify until it will be most useful. I could revise some paragraph or section forever, but I won't know if it's right until I see it in the larger chapter context. So I try to push through a whole chapter before I dismantle it. At some point, even if I'm a bit dissatisfied with it, I leave the chapter and move onto the next, so that I can revise at a higher level (two chapters together [and] eventually the whole book) later on.[1]

Like Doug, I break up my big projects into individual chapters and place them in tentative order. I start with the first and write to the end of the chapter. Inevitably, this first chapter stinks because I lack clarity on the overall structure of the book. But after five books I've learned to persevere. If I go back and start tinkering too soon, I may never make it to the end.

Reread Your First Draft Straight Through and Silence the Inner Critic

Once you have your first draft, read it straight through before you make any changes. Usually enough time has passed from when you started writing that you will have forgotten some of the things you wrote. If you start editing immediately, you may end up rewriting passages that you have already written later in the chapter, article, or book. If you print your first draft you will be less likely to make changes to the text while you read. Make notes to yourself about what needs to be changed and circle typos, bad grammar, and awkward syntax. But don't touch the electronic file until you have read the text from start to finish. When you reach the end, then go back and have at it.

Revising the awful first draft presents the hardest challenge. My own writing appalls me at this stage, and I ponder how I produced such atrocious prose. Sometimes this first round of editing takes more time than the initial writing of the whole draft, which both frustrates and exasperates. At this stage my inner critic attacks; insecurity and doubt cripple me. Emotions run wild. I ask myself: "What if this is a stupid project?" "How am I ever going to make this crap readable?" "Why the hell would anyone want to read about Bulgaria again?" Insecurity leads to distraction and procrastination. "Maybe the kitchen needs cleaning?" "Maybe I need to arrange my wardrobe by color?" In Maine, where I live most of the time, we suffer about six months of winter, so I can shovel snow, sand a path, or hack at the ice dams on the edge of my roof. My house reaps the benefit of my self-doubt. Windows get washed when I face the prospect of revising a first draft.

Books are perfect examples of commodity fetishism. Readers rarely glimpse the sweat and tears and anxieties that hide behind the sleek covers of a new book. When I read my favorite ethnographers, I deflate with the thought that I will never write a book or an article as good as these. I waste my time to produce second-rate garbage. If I silence the inner critic and stick to my guns, however, the second draft of my manuscript always improves. When I reread the manuscript after this first round of heavy editing, new questions burble up: "Is this really as bad as you thought it was?" "Are you sure there won't be an audience for this?" "How many more times can I dump ice melt on the walkway?" Slowly the inner critic falters, and I beat her back with another round of revision. By my third draft, confidence creeps back. I stand as my own worst enemy at the beginning of any project, but if I can take a deep breath and accept how badly my first drafts suck, I can finish any project. Allow yourself the freedom to suck.

Find Friendly Readers

You may want to do a third full revision before you start sharing your work, or you can find a friendly reader who has your best interests at heart. If you are writing a dissertation, a fellow graduate student might be a good first reader. If you have a good working relationship with your advisor, give it to her and tell her that it is a rough draft. If you are writing a book or an article, find a colleague who might be willing to trade work with you. Before I had tenure, I formed several small reading groups with colleagues both inside and outside of my institution. We shared drafts and discussed big picture issues like structure and organization.

If you feel paralyzed by insecurity about your writing, you can hire a professional copyeditor. Freelance copyeditors provide a variety of services, from helping you pull a whole book together to final line editing for typos and bad grammar. When I was an assistant professor, I benefitted from the ministrations of a gifted undergraduate student who worked as a writing tutor on campus. As a smart college student who cared about writing, Gen Creedon had read her fair share of bad academic books. She taught me how to organize complicated arguments so that even bored nineteen-year-olds could understand them. Gen possessed such a skilled editorial eye that I continued to work with her after she graduated, bringing her to Washington, DC, with me as an intern in the spring of 2006. I later delighted in the attentions of my copyeditor at Princeton University Press, Vicky Wilson-Schwartz. Vicky mercilessly deployed her blue pencil on *Muslim Lives in Eastern Europe*; she transformed the manuscript from a bland academic treatise into a story about ordinary people trying to make sense of a world turned upside-down.

These days I rely on the input of my partner and colleague who is an analytic philosopher. Having a reader outside of my field proves essential for ensuring that my work translates across disciplinary or sub-disciplinary borders. Scott reads with an eye for clarity and coherence and lets me get away with nothing. Sometimes I bristle at his candor, but I've learned to trust his judgment. When I gave him the first decent draft of *The Left Side of History*, he returned it to me with the words "hate it" scribbled next to the introduction in the table of contents. This was the first thing I read of his extensive comments, and my heart plummeted. I faced three courses of action: 1) get defensive and tell him that he understood nothing about ethnography; 2) hurl the manuscript off the balcony and crawl under my bed to cry; or 3) figure out what I had done wrong. After beating back the compulsion to choose either option one or two (or both), I settled for option three. Time passed and I recognized the flaws in the tone and execution of the introduction. I rewrote the whole thing.

For typos, my mom proves the best reader, because she worked as a secretary for over forty years. When I find myself perplexed by questions of content, I contact colleagues in the field and send them chunks of specific passages. For *The Left Side of History*, I read selected passages out loud to my writer's group and benefitted from the editorial comments of Sarah Braunstein. Over the years, I have built a network of people whose opinions I trust. Of course, this means I must reciprocate when other people need editorial help. Many rough drafts find their way to my desk, so I know this from experience: the best writers are the best revisers.

Invest some time in creating your own editorial networks, either by identifying friends and colleagues with whom you can trade writing or by hiring copyeditors to work with you. For thesis writers, boutique PhD or dissertation "coaches" offer help over the Internet. Although I have never used one of these services, some of them will read drafts and comment on your chapters. No matter where you find it, an extra pair of eyes on your work enhances the revision process.

Listen to Your Work

Unwieldy syntax, overused words, and typos are more easily heard than seen. When I write grant applications or letters of recommendation, I read them aloud to ensure against mistakes. These things require perfection. For longer projects, I credit Scott for introducing me to the text-to-speech function in Microsoft Word. I can highlight any passage of text and have a computer-generated voice read it back to me. In the first revision stage, I listen while reading along with a hard copy of my manuscript and make notes about organization and structure. In the line editing stage, I read along on the computer screen and make corrections directly into the electronic document. This takes a lot of time if I am dealing with a book-length manuscript, but I make the time. Even through a computer-generated voice, I can hear the tone and tenor of my writing, especially where I express ideas in a needlessly complex way. I also hear frequently repeated words that I wouldn't notice when reading. I just listened to a grant proposal that I must have read at least ten times, only to realize that I repeated the word "ongoing" four times in two paragraphs.

When I first started using the speech function, I settled for the basic Stephen Hawking voice. Now I discovered that my Apple computer allows me a choice of multiple voices. Part of *The Left Side of History* was read to me by a Scottish woman's voice called Fiona. Tessa, a South African woman's voice, read the second half. I have already decided that this book will be read by Moira (an Irish English woman's voice). For American English, Apple provides over a dozen choices, plus a whole menu of "novelty voices" like "bad news," "hysterical," "deranged," "trinoids," and "Zarvox." Zarvox might sound like something out of a bad sci-fi flick, but since final proofreading can be so tedious, why not have some fun with it?

CHAPTER 12

Find Your Process

"No electrician ever had electrician's block," read a post on my Tumblr dashboard. I laughed because I had just been pounding forehead to keyboard for lack of inspiration and was scrolling through my Tumblr feed as a way of procrastinating. Since 2011, I have hosted a Tumblr blog called "Literary Ethnography" where I ruminate on all matters relating to ethnographic writing. Today, the blog has over 6,000 "followers" (that's what Tumblr calls them), and the most common questions I receive involve writer's block and how to overcome it.

Unfortunately, no one solution exists. Everyone's brain works differently, and changing personal circumstances affect how we write at different stages in our lives. When my daughter was a preschooler and I was a single mother, I wrote my book paragraph by paragraph during the little scraps of time I salvaged between my maternal and professional responsibilities. I wrote a series of topic sentences in a Microsoft Word document and kept the file open on my computer. If my daughter got interested in an episode of Dora the Explorer, I knew I had about twenty-five minutes. I could write one or maybe two draft paragraphs. It was the most scattershot way to produce a first draft, but it was the only way I could maintain forward momentum. Now that my daughter has achieved teenager-hood, she spends hours at school, phone-gazing, or watching her favorite YouTubers. I can write whole chapters in one sitting, a luxury I never enjoyed before.

This doesn't mean that I always evade writer's block or that I don't get distracted when I sit down at the computer. I anticipate these hindrances and have developed a set of rituals to counteract them. What started out as quirks and superstitions coalesced into a defined process for seeing a project through from start to finish. My rituals work well for me, but they won't work for everyone. Each ritual must be uniquely suited to ward off specific productivity killers. As I did research for this book, I contacted some of my fellow ethnographers to ask about their writing rituals. Maybe there existed some real secrets worth sharing, a habit or trick that successful ethnographers had in common.

I made a list of my own habits and compared notes with colleagues to see if they shared any of my practices. For instance, I prefer to write when it's quiet and play loud music only when I input my line edits. Doug Rogers does almost the exact opposite:

I often write my early drafts with pretty loud music playing through headphones. There are always distractions, worries, and doubts; the blank page can be intimidating and draining, especially in the early stages. So I let familiar music (a short playlist set on repeat) take up the part of my brain that is editing too much, getting in the way of new text, or inclined to wander off and think about something else. I have "slow" and "fast" versions of this playlist to fit with my mood and how much I need to get the blood flowing—sometimes what I need to generate words on the page is pretty pounding and driving and loud, at other times it's bit more restrained. But it's not background music. It's right there, in the foreground along with the words on the screen. I know this is exactly what all of the study guides tell you never to do when you are working because it decreases concentration and increases distraction. But that's what I want—something to distract me, not from the writing but from the stuff that's getting in the way of the writing. I want my concentration to wander from the page not into whether I'm going to get the next sentence out and if it's going to be any good but, rather, into a familiar beat, lyric, or melody that carries me along, back into that next sentence, just as it did the day before, the week before. One of these songs has accompanied my writing for nearly 15 years now. Writing with these playlists often gets me to an early, ugly draft—the hardest part for me. Then I can edit. I love editing and revising. I do that in absolute silence.[1]

John Borneman says that his ritual is "discipline." He sets aside a fixed amount of time each week for "merely writing." This writing consists of "much stream-of-consciousness, free association writing that does not know where it is going" and then "lots of time editing."[2] I, too, try to write a page of "free writing," just to get in the habit of writing a certain number of words every day, a suggestion I took from Julia Cameron's influential book about creative block, *The Artist's Way*. These days I free write one page a day on a mechanical typewriter so e-mail and social media don't tempt me. But other than John, none of the ethnographers I contacted did regular "free writing."

For anthropologist Julie Hemment, writing requires a certain mindset and some creature comforts:

For me it's all about getting in the mood. In order to write, I have to feel a sense of connection with the people, places, events I describe. I have different tactics to get me there. Sometimes, I go back to my fieldnotes or audio files. On other occasions, I might remember one of my interlocutors' commentaries, their pithy/ironic remarks or analyses. My ethnographic work has always entailed collaboration (with Russian activists, scholars) and I find that channeling my colleagues in this way works especially well and gives me the sense of force and conviction I need to sit down and write.

In recent years I've become more intentional about adopting little tricks to make me *feel* like a writer (i.e., to mark that it's a shift from all the other screaming demands on my time—teaching, administrative and family commitments) and to try and make it pleasurable, special. I seek out nice new places to sit and work (not my office!); I might treat myself to a nice lunch. I like to take a swim in the morning to clear my head. This summer I even checked in to a hotel with my manuscript for a short writing retreat (just me, my laptop and a pile of chapters to edit!).

Beyond that, at the real nitty gritty level, my writing process relies upon endless rounds of editing. I work from hard copies and mark them up using a good old-fashioned pen. And, full disclosure, I have a favorite book I use to rest on (a copy of *Madeline in Paris* by Ludwig Bemelmans that was given to my daughter by one of my dearest friends and writing buddies!).[3]

Amen to Julie and her hard copies and good old-fashioned pens. I do all of my editing on paper with fountain pens, but I don't require a special place; I work everywhere, including my office. David Redmon, sociologist and ethnographic filmmaker, shared the rituals he used while writing his first book, *Bodies, Beads, and Trash*:

My one and only ritual is a rare evening with a Belgian beer (8.5%), a good book, and a computer to write. Most rituals don't work well for me so I mostly follow routines. For instance, I was teaching a 4/4 in Montreal with an 8am class while completing my first book. My morning routine consisted of waking up at 5am, drinking three to four cups of coffee while eating goat yogurt with fruit, and then I'd drink a large cup of water. I wrote from 5:30 to 7:30, and then left at 7:45am to take the metro to class. The 30 minute subway ride allowed me to read chapters from different books to generate ideas. My spouse, Ashley Sabin, was enrolled in an MFA program and during her classes I would work on my book—at her campus— while our newborn baby, Magnolia, mostly slept next to me. Ashley took breaks during class to breastfeed while I continued to write while Magnolia slept. That ritual—more of a schedule—lasted one semester.[4]

David's routine reminds me of my own schedule when I had a baby in the house, but these days I write whenever I can. I've always wanted to be one of those people who can write first thing in the morning, but I never manage it. I always choose sleep.

Amy Borovoy writes e-mails and cleans her office to get ready for writing:

> I keep a lot of notes as I write—reading notes, miscellaneous thoughts and epiphanies, and outlines. Before starting to write I look through them. Sometimes I start by sending off a couple of emails or doing some filing, just to clear my brain (and desk) a bit. Right near my printer, I keep a postcard of a Norman Rockwell illustration from *Little Women,* which is of Jo curled up on an old sofa in the attic, writing her great book. Two rats are watching her from a beam above her head.[5]

Reading notes distracts me. If I open e-mail or try to tackle the Himalayan mess on my desk, I will never write a word. Monomania sets in; whatever I start doing is what I will continue doing for hours. Always better to start writing.

After chatting with other ethnographers, I decided that compulsive editing qualified as the only habit we all had in common. Then I received this response from Olga Shevchenko:

> Not sure about writing rituals. I am a painfully slow writer but I almost never revise. This is the opposite of what most writing advice would tell you, but it just goes to show that there's no silver bullet when it comes to writing. You have to find what works for you.[6]

I could never imagine writing anything that I didn't revise at least three times before letting anyone read it, let alone sending it out for publication. But Olga is right that you have to find what works for you. Experiment and keep trying even if you fail. We all have great books and articles in us; we just need to find ways to let them out.

Since no one correct way exists to write an ethnography, I share my own process for writing books here as an example of how writing rituals can help you tackle a big project.

My Ten Steps for Writing a Book

1. Produce an imaginary table of contents

    After I've completed my research for an idea that I think will be a book, I type out an imaginary table of contents (TOC). I think about the overall argument and how to best organize the material that I will need to substantiate that argument. At this stage I make a preliminary plan about the number and the style of the chapters. For more traditional academic books, I go with fewer, but longer, chapters that are organized thematically. For projects aimed at undergraduate students or general readers, I have a greater number of short chapters and prefer a more intuitive chronological organization of the manuscript. Although this outline changes, the intellectual work that goes into its initial production helps me think through the big questions of audience, tone, and length before I start writing.

    At this stage I also consider whether I should start writing, or whether I should use this table of contents to put together a book proposal. Some ethnographers prefer to "pitch" their ideas to editors before writing the complete manuscript, and this is the way it must be done if you are interested in publishing with a trade press. Some scholars prefer to have a book under contract before they commit to a big project, and the act of writing a proposal can help clarify the goals of the book and elicit early feedback. Once I have decided to commit to a project, I move on to step two.

2. Create electronic files

    After I have the TOC, I create a separate document file for each of the chapters, as well as for the front matter, the acknowledgements, and any appendices. Then I cut and paste in any preexisting writing that I've done. I call this "found text," and I include everything that might be relevant to the chapter: journal articles, essays, book reviews, fieldnote excerpts, e-mails, outtakes from previous books, etc.

3. Write crappy first drafts

    Whether I'm building around "found text" or starting from scratch, I write a crappy first draft (CFD) of each chapter (a more polite name for Anne Lamott's SFD). I don't always do them in order, but I do not edit any individual chapter until I have CFDs of all chapters. These first drafts appall, but writing a chapter draft from start to finish without worrying about the grammar or coherence allows me to concentrate on the ideas and emotions that I want to convey. No one ever sees these drafts; I delete them all once I start revising.

4. Print out and line edit each of the chapters

    I edit by hand on paper. Editing on screen is more efficient and environmentally friendly, but it makes for lazy writing. Revising on printed pages forces me to read through an entire chapter before making changes to the electronic file. This allows me to keep the larger structure of the chapter in my head and to see how the pieces might work better in a different order. This round of revisions is tedious because it is my initial crack at correcting the serious deficiencies of the CFD.

5. Print out and revise again

    I repeat the process above. The chapters are still rough, but after this round of revisions, they start to become readable. At this stage, I also begin to focus on grammar, syntax, and narrative flow. I start watching for typos and think about topic sentences and paragraph length. I also consider how my arguments develop over the course of the chapter and what additional material I might need to substantiate my claims. Only after I have everything down on paper do I input the changes into the computer.

6. Combine the chapters into a manuscript

    After the second round of revisions, I go back to my TOC and think about the overall structure of the book. Some chapters have outgrown themselves and must be divided in two. Orphaned chapters find new homes or get cut altogether. All of the text that gets slashed is dumped into an electronic "outtakes" file. This serves as a reservoir of "found text" for future projects. All of the chapters are now combined into one electronic file.

7. Print out and line edit

    Call me a murderer of trees. I print out the entire manuscript and do a full round of line edits by hand once more. I concentrate on overall coherence and clarity and look for more material to cut. The manuscript begins to feel like something that I can share with the world without dying of shame.

8. Find friendly readers

My mom, my partner, my friends, and nonjudgmental colleagues are my first line of readers. At this point, I've usually been working too intensely and for too long on the project. I need some critical distance. Giving the whole manuscript to a few trusted interlocutors allows me to take a break and get some much-needed external input. Are my arguments clear? Is there still surplus prose? How many typos have I missed?

9. Listen to the computer read my words

Once I have incorporated all of the friendly suggestions, I use the "speech" function in Microsoft Word to have my computer read me the entire manuscript. Unwieldy syntax, overused words, and even simple typos are more easily heard than seen.

10. Complete references and send it off

The final task is to organize all of the references and the bibliography. Careful attention to the references allows me to review the overall structure of the book and think about the literature to which I will be contributing. Only once the references are in order will I begin to contact editors. At this point, the manuscript is ready for blind review. I say a little prayer, send it off, and start work on my next project.

Ten Steps—An analogue infographic of the author's ten steps for writing a book.

Conclusion

Writing is a skill, and skills develop with time and practice. There exists no magic formula for writing well, and you should not wait to be a "good" writer before you start writing. Push forward with your projects no matter what your writing ability. Writer's block happens, but you can manage it with the right tools.

The chapters in this book have highlighted various strategies you can use to write a clear and accessible ethnography, one comprehensible to an audience beyond your small circle of scholarly peers. These are:

1. *Choose a subject you love*—If you are early enough in your process, research something that excites you, and if it's already too late, then think of ways to write a really great book with the scholarship that you've already done.
2. *Put yourself into the data*—Don't be afraid to write yourself into your ethnography, especially when describing your methodology or trying to link disparate parts of your fieldwork.
3. *Incorporate ethnographic detail*—Show, don't tell. Treat your ethnographic data as more than substantiating evidence. Pay attention to people and what makes them unique.
4. *Describe places and events*—Use your descriptions of geographies and happenings as metaphors for the arguments in your manuscript. Transport your readers into the world of your informants.

5. *Integrate your theory* — Don't alienate your reader with a wall of theoretical rumination. Learn to interweave your ethnographic data with relevant insights from the extant literature.

6. *Embrace dialogue* — Take detailed fieldnotes and render your informants' words into literary dialogue. Use dialogue to add narrative variation to your manuscript.

7. *Include images* — Select images that complement your ethnographic data. Include as many as your publisher will allow. Make sure you get permissions.

8. *Minimize scientism* — If possible, avoid unnecessary jargon and use endnotes instead of author-date citation.

9. *Unclutter your prose* — Learn to write lean. Choose simple words over complex ones, keep subjects and verbs together, watch the passive voice, and beware the adverb and adjective.

10. *Master good grammar and syntax* — Use the English language well. Read style guides and emulate ethnographers you admire. Avoid weak verbs.

11. *Revise* — Write first drafts straight through, and then revise the heck out of them. Find friendly readers. Listen to your work read aloud.

12. *Find your process* — Invent writing rituals that work for you.

When you are junior, implementing all of this advice might prove difficult. Journals maintain style rules, and senior colleagues expect your work to conform to disciplinary norms. Sometimes first books need to be specialized books aimed at a small audience of scholars who might serve on your tenure committee. By all means, do what you must do to establish your reputation as a serious scholar, but don't think that being obtuse makes you sound smarter. If your ideas are original and your research is sound, you can write texts that speak to audiences beyond your eventual tenure reviewers. Students, informants, and even your colleagues will thank you.

Acknowledgments

I never thought I would write a book about writing. This project was born of ire and frustration, and I am grateful to the wide variety of colleagues, friends, and students who encouraged me to channel my all-too-frequent rants against *academese* into this project. It is one thing to notice and complain about the proliferation of bad prose in ethnographic writing, and another thing to try to do something about it. Perhaps I am fighting a losing battle, but at least I can say that I tried to fight.

I want to thank Jean Lave and Carol Stack who taught my qualitative methods courses at UC Berkeley so many eons ago, as well as Ken Wissoker, Fred Appel, and Courtney Berger, my editors at Duke and Princeton University Presses, who encouraged me to write ethnographies that everyone could read. I am especially thankful to Mary Laur at the University of Chicago Press for believing in the project, and to the three reviewers for their constructive criticism: Alma Gottlieb, Jonathan Wynn, and Michelle Morano.

My students at Bowdoin College were always forthcoming with their opinions on the texts I assigned them to read, and their insights allowed me to consider the factors that make academic work accessible. My Bowdoin colleagues also deserve gratitude for their various forms of support for me over the years, but especially my immediate colleagues Jennifer Scanlon, Susan Faludi, Frances Gouda, and Anne Clifford, who held the fort while I was away on sabbatical. I wrote the majority of this book during the summer and the early fall of my leave from Bowdoin College, which supported me with a Faculty Leave Supplement so that I could accept a Senior External Fellowship at the Freiburg Institute for Advanced Studies (FRIAS) in Germany for the 2014–2015 academic year. Many thanks to the academic staff of FRIAS—Britta Küst, Petra Fischer, Helen Pert, Nikolaus Binder—and especially the directors, Prof. Dr. Bernd Kortmann and Dr. Carsten Dose, who made my research stay in Freiburg so delightful. I am grateful to Jörn and Marlies Ambs for being such lovely neighbors at Am Moosgraben 5. Finally, I would also like to acknowledge my generous colleagues who shared their knowledge and expertise about moving from notes to narrative.

Although she'll never be able to read this, I feel compelled to at least acknowledge the essential contribution of my basset hound, Daisy, who came with me to Germany and kept me company while I wrote this book. Aside from the occasional demand for food, water, and walks, Daisy was a steadfast companion during my writing binges. I'd also like to thank my partner, Scott, for being patient and supportive, and for being such an excellent "friendly reader." Joan Didion once said, "Grammar is a piano I play by ear." For me, grammar is a partner who never fails to correct me when I mix up "lay" and "lie." My daughter has recently joined the grammar police, which now makes her a fantastic proofreader as well as a constant source of amusement and inspiration. In addition to their pronoun vigilance, my family put up with my writing idiosyncrasies and tolerated my monomania. I'm amazed they still want me around.

Finally, the members of my writing group back in Maine—Annie Finch, Pope Brock, and especially Sarah Braunstein—broke me out of my academic cocoon. All three of them taught the craft of writing in American MFA programs, and over the three years that we met to share our work, I gleaned much knowledge from their constructive criticisms. More importantly, I treasured their support and friendship. It is to Annie, Pope, and Sarah that I dedicate this book.

Notes

INTRODUCTION

1. See, for instance, Ghodsee, "When Research becomes Intelligence."
2. Givlier, "University Press Publishing in the United States," online.
3. Van Maanen, *Tales of the Field*, 147.

CHAPTER 1

1. Michael Herzfeld, "Passionate Serendipity: From the Acropolis to the Golden Mount," in *The Restless Anthropologist: New Fieldsites, New Visions*, ed. Alma Gottlieb (Chicago: University of Chicago Press, 2008), 100–22.
2. Jerome Groopman, "The Victory of Oliver Sacks," *New York Review of Books* LXII, no. 9 (May 21–June 2, 2015): 6.

CHAPTER 2

1. Guenther, *Making Their Place*, 141.
2. Stoller, *Fusion of the Worlds*.
3. Anderson, *Code of the Street*, 11.
4. Van Maanen, *Tales of the Field*, 175.
5. See Jacob Brogan's April 1, 2015, essay on "Why Scientists Need to Give Up on the Passive Voice" on Slate.com.
6. Behar, *Traveling Heavy*, 6.
7. Wacquant, *Body and Soul*, 4.
8. McDermott, *Working-Class White*, 108.
9. Narayan, *Alive in the Writing*, 96.
10. Borneman, *Syrian Episodes*, ix.
11. On the value of direct experience, also see the edited collection by Sarah Davis and Melvin Konner, *Being There*.
12. Borneman, *Syrian Episodes*, 150.
13. Bourgois, *In Search of Respect*, 318.

CHAPTER 3

1. Clifford Geertz, "Deep Play," 1–37.
2. Personal e-mail communication with Elaine Weiner, May 7, 2014.
3. Emerson, Fritz, and Shaw, *Writing Ethnographic Fieldnotes*.
4. Aristotle, *Poetics*, online.
5. Lacy, *Blue-Chip Black*, 1.

CHAPTER 4

1. Gottlieb and Graham, *Parallel Worlds*, 3.
2. Ghodsee, *The Red Riviera*, 1.
3. Anderson, *Code of the Street*, 15.
4. Dunn, *Privatizing Poland*, 72.
5. Warner, *The Living and the Dead*, 1.

CHAPTER 5

1. Personal e-mail communication with John Borneman, April 27, 2014.
2. Personal e-mail communication with Amy Borovoy, May 6, 2014.
3. Personal e-mail communication with Julie Hemment, August 16, 2014.
4. Personal e-mail communication with Olga Shevchenko, April 27, 2014.
5. Fields, *Risky Lessons*, 138.
6. Borneman, *Syrian Episodes*, xii.
7. Aizenman and Kletzer, "The Life Cycle of Scholars and Papers in Economics."
8. Personal e-mail communication with Olga Shevchenko, April 27, 2014.
9. Personal e-mail communication with Julie Hemment, August 16, 2014.
10. Personal e-mail communication with Doug Rogers, September 9, 2014.

CHAPTER 6

1. Stoller, *Fusion of the Worlds*, 12.
2. Kahn, *Privilege*, 102.

CHAPTER 7

1. Harper, *Working Knowledge*, 122–23.

CHAPTER 8

1. Mills, *The Sociological Imagination*, 27.
2. Ibid.
3. Sokal, "Transgressing the Boundaries," 217–52.
4. See http://www.elsewhere.org/pomo/
5. See http://writing-program.uchicago.edu/toys/randomsentence/write-sentence.htm

6. Williams, *Style*, *10*.
7. Kerins, "The Academic Con-Men."
8. Dennett, *Breaking the Spell*.
9. American Anthropological Association, *Style Guide* (2009), online: http://www.aaanet.org/publications/style_guide.pdf

CHAPTER 9

1. Strunk and White, *Elements of Style*, 23.
2. Orwell, "Politics and the English Language," online.
3. Zinsser, *On Writing Well*, 177.
4. Owen, "In Defense of the Least Publishable Unit."
5. Rovit and Waldhorn. *Hemingway and Faulkner in Their Time*, 162.
6. Oppenheimer, "Consequences of Erudite Vernacular."
7. Ibid., 152.

CHAPTER 10

1. Provost, *100 Ways to Improve Your Writing*, 60–61.

CHAPTER 11

1. Personal e-mail communication with Doug Rogers, September 9, 2014.

CHAPTER 12

1. Personal e-mail communication with Doug Rogers, September 9, 2014.
2. Personal e-mail communication with John Borneman, April 27, 2014.
3. Personal e-mail communication with Julie Hemment, August 16, 2014.
4. Personal e-mail communication with David Redmon, May 6, 2014.
5. Personal e-mail communication with Amy Borovoy, May 6, 2014.
6. Personal e-mail communication with Olga Shevchenko, April 27, 2014.

Suggested Reading and Bibliography

I provide a selection of books that might be of use to ethnographers hoping to improve their writing. Although there are many excellent examples of ethnographic writing published in journals such as *Ethnography*, *Journal of Contemporary Ethnography*, *American Ethnologist*, and *Anthropology and Humanism*, I have limited the resources listed here to published books for the sake of brevity. This list is by no means comprehensive, but merely a sample of the many useful texts out there.

SELECTED GENERAL BOOKS ABOUT WRITING

Chicago Manual of Style. 16th ed. Chicago: University of Chicago Press, 2010.

Cameron, Julia. *The Artist's Way: A Spiritual Path to Higher Creativity*, 10th Anniversary ed. Jeremy P. Tarcher/Putnam, 2002.

Goldberg, Natalie. *Writing Done the Bones*, expanded ed. Boston: Shambhala, 1995.

Hale, Constance. *Sin and Syntax: How to Craft Wickedly Effective Prose.* New York: Broadway Books, 2001.

Lamott, Anne. *Bird by Bird: Some Instructions on Writing and Life.* New York: Anchor, 1995.

Orwell, George. *Why I Write.* Penguin Great Ideas. New York: Penguin Books, 2005.

Pinker, Steven. *The Sense of Style: The Thinking Person's Guide to Writing in the 21st Century.* New York: Viking, 2014.

Provost, Gary. *100 Ways to Improve Your Writing.* Signet, 1985.

Strunk, William, and E. B. White. *The Elements of Style*, 4th ed. London: Longman, 1999.

Sword, Helen. *Stylish Academic Writing.* Cambridge: Harvard University Press, 2012.

136   Suggested Reading and Bibliography

Williams, Joseph. *Style: Lessons in Clarity and Grace*, 11th ed. London: Longman, 2013.
Zinsser, William. *On Writing Well: The Classic Guide to Writing Nonfiction*, 30th Anniversary ed. New York: Harper Perennial, 2006.

SELECTED GENERAL BOOKS ABOUT WRITING
AND PUBLISHING IN THE SOCIAL SCIENCES

Becker, Howard. *Tricks of the Trade: How to Think about Your Research While You're Doing it.* Chicago: University of Chicago Press, 1998.
Becker, Howard. *Writing for Social Scientists: How to Start and Finish Your Thesis, Book, or Article*, 2nd ed. Chicago: University of Chicago Press, 2007.
Becker, Howard. *Telling About Society.* Chicago: University of Chicago Press, 2007.
Germano, William. *From Dissertation to Book*, 2nd ed. Chicago: University of Chicago Press, 2013.
Germano, William. *Getting it Published: A Guide for Scholars and Anyone Else Serious about Serious Books.* Chicago: University of Chicago Press, 2008.

SELECTED BOOKS ON ETHNOGRAPHIC METHODS AND WRITING

Boellstorff, Tom, Bonnie Nardi, Celia Pearce, and T. L. Taylor. *Ethnography and Virtual Worlds: A Handbook of Method.* Princeton: Princeton University Press, 2012.
Borneman, John, and Abdellah Hammoudi. *Being There: The Fieldwork Encounter and the Making of Truth.* Berkeley: University of California Press, 2009.
Clifford, James, and George Marcus. *Writing Culture: The Poetics and Politics of Ethnography*, 25th anniversary ed. Berkeley: University of California Press, 2010.
Emerson, Robert, Rachel Fritz, and Linda Shaw. *Writing Ethnographic Fieldnotes*, 2nd ed. Chicago: University of Chicago Press, 2011.
Goodall, H. L. *Writing the New Ethnography.* Maryland: AltaMira Press, 2000.
Gottlieb, Alma, ed. *The Restless Anthropologist: New Fieldsites, New Visions.* Chicago: University of Chicago Press, 2008.
Lassiter, Luke. *The Chicago Guide to Collaborative Ethnography.* Chicago: University of Chicago Press, 2005.
Narayan, Kirin. *Alive in the Writing: Crafting Ethnography in the Company of Chekhov.* Chicago: University of Chicago Press, 2012.
Van Maanen, John. *Tales of the Field: On Writing Ethnography*, 2nd ed. Chicago: University of Chicago Press, 2011.

SELECTED ETHNOGRAPHIC BOOKS THAT EVERYONE CAN READ
Note: An asterisk denotes a book that has won the Victor Turner Award in Ethnographic Writing from the Society of Humanistic Anthropology.

Abu-Lughod, Lila. *Writing Women's Worlds: Bedouin Stories.* Berkeley: University of California Press, 1993.*

Allison, Anne. *Nightwork: Sexuality, Pleasure, and Corporate Masculinity in a Tokyo Hostess Club.* Chicago: University of Chicago Press, 1994.

Anderson, Elijah. *Code of the Street: Decency, Violence, and the Code of the Inner City.* New York: W. W. Norton, 1999.

Aretxaga, Begoña. *Shattering Silence: Women, Nationalism, and Political Subjectivity in Northern Ireland.* Princeton: Princeton University Press, 2007.

Bashkow, Ira. *The Meaning of Whitemen: Race and Modernity in the Orokaiva Cultural World.* Chicago: University of Chicago Press, 2006.*

Basso, Keith H. *Wisdom Sits in Places: Landscape and Language among the Western Apache.* Albuquerque: University of New Mexico Press, 1996.*

Behar, Ruth. *The Vulnerable Observer: Anthropology that Breaks Your Heart.* Boston: Beacon Press, 1997.

Behar, Ruth. *Translated Woman: Crossing the Border with Esperanza's Story.* Boston: Beacon Press, 2003.

Behar, Ruth. *An Island Called Home: Returning to Cuba.* New Brunswick: Rutgers University Press, 2007.

Behar, Ruth. *Traveling Heavy: A Memoir between Journeys.* Durham: Duke University Press, 2013.

Biehl, João. *Vita: Life in a Zone of Social Abandonment.* Berkeley: University of California Press, 2013.

Biehl, João. *Will to Live: AIDS Therapies and the Politics of Survival.* Princeton: Princeton University Press, 2009.

Boddy, Janice. *Wombs and Alien Spirits: Women, Men, and the Zar Cult in Northern Sudan.* Madison: University of Wisconsin Press, 1989.

Boellstorff, Tom. *Coming of Age in Second Life: An Anthropologist Explores the Virtually Human.* Princeton: Princeton University Press, 2010.

Bogle, Kathleen. *Hooking Up: Sex, Dating, and Relationships on Campus.* New York: New York University Press, 2008.

Borneman, John. *Syrian Episodes: Sons, Fathers, and an Anthropologist in Aleppo.* Princeton: Princeton University Press, 2007.

Borovoy, Amy. *The Too-Good Wife: Alcohol, Codependency, and the Politics of Nurturance in Postwar Japan.* Berkeley: University of California Press, 2005.

Bourgois, Philippe. *In Search of Respect: Selling Crack in El Barrio*. Cambridge: Cambridge University Press, 2003.

Bourgois, Phillipe. *Righteous Dopefiend*. Berkeley: University of California Press, 2009.

Briggs, Jean L. *Inuit Morality Play: The Emotional Education of a Three-Year-Old*. New Haven: Yale University Press, 1998.*

Brown, Karen McCarthy. *Mama Lola: A Vodou Priestess in Brooklyn*. Berkeley: University of California Press, 2011.*

Chernoff, John M. *Hustling Is Not Stealing: Stories of an African Bar Girl*. Chicago: University of Chicago Press, 2003.*

Cohen, Lawrence. *No Aging in India: Alzheimer's, The Bad Family, and Other Modern Things*. Berkeley: University of California Press, 2000.*

Cruikshank, Julie. *Do Glaciers Listen? Local Knowledge, Colonial Encounters, and Social Imagination*. Seattle: University of Washington Press, 2005.*

Danforth, Loring, and Riki von Boeschoten. *Children of the Greek Civil War: Refugees and the Politics of Memory*. Chicago: University of Chicago Press, 2011.

Deeb, Lara. *An Enchanted Modern: Gender and Public Piety in Shi'i Lebanon*. Princeton: Princeton University Press, 2006.

Delany, Carol. *The Seed and the Soil: Gender and Cosmology in Turkish Village Society*. Berkeley: University of California Press, 1991.

Desjarlais, Robert. *Shelter Blues: Sanity and Selfhood among the Homeless*. Philadelphia: University of Pennsylvania Press, 1997.*

Dettwyler, Katheryn. *Dancing with Skeletons: Life and Death in West Africa*. Long Grove, IL: Waveland Press, 1993.

Duneier, Mitchell. *Sidewalk*. New York: Farrar, Straus and Girox, 1999.

Dunn, Elizabeth. *Privatizing Poland: Baby Food, Big Business, and the Remaking of Labor*. Ithaca: Cornell University Press, 2004.

Edmonds, Alexander. *Pretty Modern: Beauty, Sex, and Plastic Surgery in Brazil*. Durham: Duke University Press, 2010.

Engelke, Matthew. *A Problem of Presence: Beyond Scripture in an African Church*. Berkeley: University of California Press, 2007.*

Feld, Steven. *Sound and Sentiment: Birds, Weeping, Poetics, and Song in Kaluli Expression*, 3rd ed. Durham: Duke University Press, 2012.

Fields, Jessica. *Risky Lessons: Sex Education and Social Inequality*. Brunswick, NJ: Rutgers University Press, 2008.

Flueckiger, Joyce Burkhalter. *Amma's Healing Room: Gender and Vernacular Islam in South India*. Bloomington: Indiana University Press, 2006.

Freeman, Carla. *High Tech and High Heels in the Global Economy: Women, Work, and Pink Collar Identities in the Caribbean*. Durham: Duke University Press, 2000.

Garcia, Angela. *The Pastoral Clinic: Addiction and Dispossession along the Rio Grande*. Berkeley: University of California Press, 2010.*

Gaudio, Rudolf Pell. *Allah Made Us: Sexual Outlaws in an Islamic African City*. Hoboken, NJ: Wiley-Blackwell, 2009.

Goldman, Michael. *Imperial Nature: The World Bank and Struggles for Social Justice in the Age of Globalization*. New Haven: Yale University Press, 2006.

Gomberg-Munoz, Ruth. *Labor and Legality: An Ethnography of a Mexican Immigrant Network*. New York: Oxford University Press, 2010.

Gottlieb, Alma, and Philip Graham. *Braided Worlds*. Chicago: University of Chicago Press, 2012.

Gottlieb, Alma, and Philip Graham. *Parallel Worlds: An Anthropologist and a Writer Encounter Africa*. Chicago: University of Chicago Press, 1994.*

Gottlieb, Alma. *The Afterlife Is Where We Come From*. Chicago: University of Chicago Press, 2004.

Grasseni, Cristina. *Developing Skill, Developing Vision: Practices of Locality at the Foot of the Alps*. Oxford: Berghahn Publishers, 2009.

Guenther, Katja M. *Making Their Place: Feminism after Socialism in Eastern Germany*. Palo Alto: Stanford University Press, 2010.

Harper, Douglas. *Good Company*. Chicago: University Of Chicago Press, 1982.

Harper, Douglas. *Working Knowledge: Skill and Community in a Small Shop*. Chicago: University of Chicago Press, 1987.

Heatherington, Tracey. *Wild Sardinia: Indigeneity and the Global Dreamtimes of Environmentalism*. Seattle: University of Washington Press, 2010.*

Hemment, Julie. *Empowering Women in Russia: Activism, Aid, and NGOs*. Bloomington: Indiana University Press, 2007.

Herzfeld, Michael. *Evicted From Eternity: The Restructuring of Modern Rome*. Chicago: University of Chicago Press, 2009.

Herzfeld, Michael. *The Body Impolitic: Artisans and Artifice in the Global Hierarchy of Value*. Chicago: University of Chicago Press, 2003.

Ho, Karen. *Liquidated: An Ethnography of Wall Street*. Durham: Duke University Press, 2009.

Holmes, Seth. *Fresh Fruit, Broken Bodies: Migrant Farmworkers in the United States*. Berkeley: University of California Press, 2013.

Holmes-Eber, Paula. *Daughters of Tunis: Women, Family, and Networks in a Muslim City*. Boulder, CO: Westview Press, 2002.

Jain, S. Lochlann. *Malignant: How Cancer Becomes Us*. Berkeley: University of California Press, 2013.*

Kahn, Shamus Rahman. *Privilege: The Making of an Adolescent Elite at St. Paul's School*. Princeton: Princeton University Press, 2011.

Klima, Alan. *The Funeral Casino: Meditation, Massacre, and Exchange with the Dead in Thailand*. Princeton: Princeton University Press, 2002.*

Lacy, Karyn. *Blue-Chip Black: Race, Class, and Status in the New Black Middle Class*. Berkeley: University of California Press, 2007.

Lee, Ching Kwan. *Gender and the South China Miracle: Two Worlds of Factory Women*. Berkeley: University of California Press, 1998.

Livingston, Julie. *Improvising Medicine: An African Oncology Ward in an Emerging Cancer Epidemic*. Durham: Duke University Press, 2012.*

Luhrmann, Tanya M. *Of Two Minds: An Anthropologist Looks at American Psychiatry*. New York: Alfred A. Knopf/Random House, 2000.*

Maggi, Wynne. *Our Women Are Free: Gender and Ethnicity in the Hindukush*. Ann Arbor: University of Michigan Press, 2001.

Maurer, Bill. *Mutual Life, Limited: Islamic Banking, Alternative Currencies, Lateral Reason*. Princeton: Princeton University Press, 2005.*

McDermott, Monica. *Working-Class White: The Making and Unmaking of Race Relations*. Berkeley: University of California Press, 2006.

Narayan, Kirin. *Storytellers, Saints, and Scoundrels: Folk Narrative in Hindu Religious Teaching*. Philadelphia: University of Pennsylvania Press, 1989.*

Ortner, Sherry. *Not Hollywood: Independent Film at the Twilight of the American Dream*. Durham: Duke University Press, 2013.

Panourgiá, Neni. *Dangerous Citizens: The Greek Left and the Terror of the State*. New York: Fordham University Press, 2009.*

Paxson, Heather. *The Life of Cheese: Crafting Food and Value in America*. Berkeley: University of California Press, 2012.

Perez, Gina. *The Near Northwest Side Story: Migration, Displacement, and Puerto Rican Families*. Berkeley: University of California Press, 2004.

Price, Richard. *Travels with Tooy: History, Memory, and the African Imagination*. Chicago: University of Chicago Press, 2007.*

Rogers, Doug. *The Old Faith and the Russian Land: A Historical Ethnography of Ethics in the Urals*. Ithaca: Cornell University Press, 2009.

Scheper-Hughes, Nancy. *Saints, Scholars, and Schizophrenics: Mental Illness in Rural Ireland*, 20th Anniversary ed. Berkeley: University of California Press, 2001.

Sharp, Henry S. *Loon: Memory, Meaning, and Reality in a Northern Dene Community*. Lincoln: University of Nebraska Press, 2004.*

Stack, Carol B. *Call to Home: African Americans Reclaim the Rural South*. New York: Basic Books, 1996.*

Stack, Carol. *All Our Kin: Strategies for Survival in a Black Community*. New York: Basic Books, 1983.

Steedly, Mary Margaret. *Hanging without a Rope: Narrative Experience in Colonial and Postcolonial Karoland*. Princeton: Princeton University Press, 2007.*

Stoller, Paul. *Embodying Colonial Memories: Spirit Possession, Power, and the Hauka in West Africa*. New York: Routledge, 1995.

Stoller, Paul. *Fusion of the Worlds: An Ethnography of Possession among the Songhay of Niger*. Chicago: University of Chicago Press, 1989.

Striffler, Steve. *Chicken: The Dangerous Transformation of America's Favorite Food*. New Haven: Yale University Press, 2007.

Taussig, Michael. *Law in a Lawless Land: Diary of a Limpieza in Colombia*. Chicago: University of Chicago Press, 2005.

Tedlock, Dennis. *Days from a Dream Almanac*. Champaign, IL: University of Illinois Press, 1989.*

Varzi, Roxanne. *Warring Souls: Youth, Media, and Martyrdom in Post-Revolution Iran*. Durham: Duke University Press, 2006.

Verdery, Katherine. *The Vanishing Hectare: Property and Value in Postsocialist Transylvania*. Ithaca: Cornell University Press, 2003.

Wacquant, Loïc. *Body and Soul: Notebooks of an Apprentice Boxer*. New York: Oxford University Press, 2004.

Wafer, Jim. *The Taste of Blood: Spirit Possession in Brazilian Candomble*. Philadelphia: University of Pennsylvania Press, 1991.*

Warner, W. Lloyd. *The Living and the Dead: A Study of the Symbolic Life of the Americas*. Yankee City Series, vol. 5. New Haven: Yale University Press, 1959.

Weiner, Elaine. *Market Dreams: Gender, Class, and Capitalism in the Czech Republic*. Ann Arbor: University of Michigan Press, 2007.

Wiener, Margaret. *Visible and Invisible Realms: Power, Magic, and Colonial Conquest in Bali*. Chicago: University of Chicago Press, 1995.*

REFERENCES (NOT ALREADY CITED ABOVE)

Aizenman, J., and Kenneth Kletzer. "The Life Cycle of Scholars and Papers in Economics—The "Citation Death Tax." NBER Working Paper No. 13891, March 2008. http://www.nber.org/papers/w13891.pdf.

Aristotle. *Poetics*. http://classics.mit.edu/Aristotle/poetics.html.

Baker, Nicholson. *The Mezzanine*. New York: Grove Press, 2010.

Brogan, Jacob. "Why Scientists Need to Give Up on the Passive Voice." Slate .com (April 1, 2015). http://www.slate.com/blogs/future_tense/2015/04/01 /scientists_should_stop_writing_in_the_passive_voice.html.

Chow, Rey. *The Age of the World Target: Self-Referentiality in War, Theory, and Comparative Work*. Durham: Duke University Press, 2006.

Davis, Sarah, and Melvin Konner. *Being There: Learning to Live Cross-Culturally*. Cambridge: Harvard University Press, 2011.

Dennett, Daniel. *Breaking the Spell: Religion as a Natural Phenomenon*. New York: Penguin Books, 2007.

Du, Shanshan. *Chopsticks Only Work in Paris: Gender Unity and Gender Equality among the Lahu in Southwest China.* New York: Columbia University Press, 2002.

Geertz, Clifford. "Deep Play: Notes on a Balinese Cockfight." *Daedalus* 101, no. 1 (Winter 1972): 1–37.

Ghodsee, Kristen. "When Research becomes Intelligence: Feminist Anthropology, Ethnographic Fieldwork and the Human Terrain System." *Feminist Formations* (formerly the *National Women's Studies Association Journal*), 23, no. 2 (Summer 2011b): 160–85.

Ghodsee, Kristen. *Lost in Transition: Ethnographies of Everyday Life after Communism.* Durham: Duke University Press, 2011a.

Ghodsee, Kristen. *Muslim Lives in Eastern Europe: Gender, Ethnicity and the Transformation of Islam in Postsocialist Bulgaria.* Princeton: Princeton University Press, 2009.

Ghodsee, Kristen. *The Left Side of History: World War II and the Unfulfilled Promise of Communism in Eastern Europe.* Durham: Duke University Press, 2015.

Ghodsee, Kristen. *The Red Riviera: Gender, Tourism and Postsocialism on the Black Sea.* Durham: Duke University Press, 2005.

Givlier, Peter. "University Press Publishing in the United States." http://www.aaup net.org/about-aaup/about-university-presses/history-of-university-presses#sthash.sp0YNRiz.dpufohn.

Gladwell, Malcolm. *Blink: The Power of Thinking Without Thinking.* Boston: Back Bay Books/Little, Brown, 2007.

Gladwell, Malcolm. *The Tipping Point: How Little Things Can Make a Big Difference.* Boston: Back Bay Books/Little, Brown, 2002.

Grindal, Bruce. "The Spirit of Humanistic Anthropology." *Anthropology and Humanism* 18, no. 2 (1993): 46–47.

Kerins, Francis J. "The Academic Con-Men: Advice to Young College Professors." *Journal of Higher Education* 32, no. 6 (1961).

Kristof, Nicholas, and Sheryl WuDunn. *Half the Sky: Turning Oppression into Opportunities for Women.* New York: Vintage, 2010.

Levitt, Steven, and Stephen J. Dubner. *Freakonomics: A Rogue Economist Explores the Hidden Side of Everything.* New York: William Morrow, 2005.

Mahmood, Saba. *The Politics of Piety: The Islamic Revival and the Feminist Subject.* Princeton: Princeton University Press, 2011.

Mills, C. Wright. *The Sociological Imagination,* 40th Anniversary ed. New York: Oxford University Press, 2000.

Newton, Esther. *Mother Camp: Female Impersonators in America.* Chicago: University of Chicago Press, 1972.

Oppenheimer, Daniel M. "Consequences of Erudite Vernacular Utilized Irrespective of Necessity: Problems with Using Long Words Needlessly." *Applied Cognitive Psychology* 20 (2006): 139–56.

Orwell, George. "Politics and the English Language" (1946). www.npr.org/blogs /... /Politics_and_the_English_Language-1.pdf.

Owen, Whitney J. "In Defense of the Least Publishable Unit." *The Chronicle of Higher Education* (February 9, 2004). http://chronicle.com/article/In-Defense -of-the-Least/44761.

Piketty, Thomas. *Capital in the Twenty-First Century.* Cambridge: Harvard University Press, 2014.

Putnam, Robert. *Bowling Alone: The Collapse and Revival of American Community.* New York: Touchstone Books, 2000.

Riesman, David. *The Lonely Crowd: A Study of the Changing American Character,* revised ed. New Haven: Yale University Press, 2001.

Rovit, Earl, and Arther Waldhorn. *Hemingway and Faulkner in Their Time.* Continuum, 2006.

Sokal, Alan. "Transgressing the Boundaries: Toward a Transformative Hermeneutics of Quantum Gravity." *Social Text* 46/47 (1996): 217–52.

Stern, Pamela, and Lisa Stevenson. *Critical Inuit Studies: An Anthology of Contemporary Artic Ethnography.* Lincoln: University of Nebraska Press, 2006.

Valentine, David. *Imagining Transgender: An Ethnography of a Category.* Durham: Duke University Press, 2007.

Index